SIMPLY STYLISH
MEALS
IN
15 MINUTES

CAROLYN HUMPHRIES

LONDON • NEW YORK • TORONTO • SYDNEY

foulsham

The Publishing House, Bennetts Close,
Cippenham, Slough, Berkshire, SL1 5AP, England

ISBN 0-572-02468-1

Copyright © 1999 W. Foulsham & Co. Ltd

Printed in Great Britain by Cox & Wyman Ltd, Reading

CONTENTS

❁

INTRODUCTION

We all seem to live life in the fast lane these days with little or no time to cook.

But for many of us, food is important – a pleasure, not just a necessity. It's no good looking at recipe books with endless lists of unfamiliar ingredients only to discover, even if you scour the world for them, that they take an age to prepare and cook. You need a handy little tome, bursting with easy-to-prepare meals made from fresh, simple ingredients that look and taste exquisite. And here it is!

In this book, I've created a whole range of mouth-watering starters, main courses and puds. You don't have to be a first-class chef to make them and they don't take an eternity to cook (if at all).

And if you just want a quick bite, you needn't settle for a can of beans on toast any more. There's a whole chapter on delicious snacks and one on quick bakes to set your taste buds tingling.

When you've dipped into this book a few times, I'm sure you'll agree that the most wonderful meals don't have to be difficult or time-consuming to prepare. The very best are quick and easy 15 minute meals!

NOTES ON THE RECIPES

- When following a recipe, use either metric, imperial or American measures, never a combination.

- All spoon measures are level: 1 tsp = 5 ml
                                   1 tbsp = 15 ml

- Eggs are medium unless otherwise stated.

- Use any good-quality light oil, like sunflower or groundnut (peanut), unless olive oil is specifically called for.

- All preparation and cooking times are approximate.

- Always wash, peel, core and seed, if necessary, all fresh produce before use.

- Always use fresh herbs, unless dried are specified. You can substitute dried herbs, but use only half the stated quantity as they are very pungent.

- Always preheat the oven (unless using a fan-assisted oven) and cook on the centre shelf unless otherwise stated.

BUILDING A STORECUPBOARD

When we all lead such busy lives, it is not just the cooking that we have little time for, it's the planning and shopping as well. The easiest way to minimise wasted time is to do some advance planning. An hour or two spent sorting out a storecupboard of basics, then a few minutes each week before you go shopping makes all the difference. Of course, once you get into the system, you'll want to personalise your own storecupboard list.

First, buy in a basic stock of the items below. You don't have to buy them all at once, you can collect them over the course of a few weeks. Then keep a shopping list and jot down any items as you use them or notice that you are getting to the bottom of a jar or packet. Before you do your weekly shop, spend a few moments thinking about how many people you have to make meals for during the course of the week and choose the basics on which you are going to base your meals. That way, even if you have only decided it will be chicken one day and sausages the next, you know where to start looking for an interesting way of serving them – and to find that, just turn to the index.

Cans, Bottles and Packets
- Chick peas
- Red kidney beans
- Passata (sieved tomatoes)
- Tomatoes
- Tomato purée (paste)
- Honey
- Lemon juice
- Olive oil
- Sunflower oil
- Wine vinegar
- Cornflour (cornstarch)
- Plain (all-purpose) flour
- Baking powder
- Pasta
- Long-grain rice
- Caster (superfine) sugar
- Stuffing mix

Herbs, Spices and Seasonings
- Salt and black peppercorns for grinding
- Mustard
- Dried mixed herbs
- Soy sauce
- Tabasco sauce
- Worcestershire sauce
- Stock cubes
- Spices: mixed (apple-pie) spice, cinnamon, cumin, coriander, curry powder, ground ginger, nutmeg, paprika, chilli or cayenne

Vegetables
- Potatoes
- Onions
- Garlic
- Carrots
- Salad stuffs

Fridge
- Eggs
- Cheddar cheese
- Butter or margarine
- Milk
- Mayonnaise
- Orange juice

Freezer
- Bread
- Pastry (paste)
- Peas
- Parsley, chopped
- Prawns
- Fish fillets
- Chicken portions
- Lamb chops or steaks
- Pork chops or steaks
- Sausages
- Minced beef or lamb

SOUPS

◎

*Soups are a good choice before less
substantial main courses. But they also make
delicious light meals, served with crusty
bread and followed by a cheese board and
fresh fruit.*

*Be adventurous in adapting recipes.
Substitute frozen peas for the spinach and
broad beans in Green Velvet Soup, use cream
instead of milk and add lots of fresh mint to
make a delicious minted pea soup.*

Chilled Cucumber Soup with Dill

SERVES 4	METRIC	IMPERIAL	AMERICAN
Cucumber	1	1	1
Salt			
Dried dill (dill weed)	10 ml	2 tsp	2 tsp
Cider vinegar or wine vinegar	30 ml	2 tbsp	2 tbsp
Pepper			
Plain yoghurt	300 ml	½ pt	1¼ cups
Cold milk	300 ml	½ pt	1¼ cups

1 Cut four thin slices from the cucumber and reserve for garnish. Grate the remainder into a bowl.

2 Sprinkle with salt, stir and leave to stand for 10 minutes.

3 Squeeze out all the moisture and drain off.

4 Stir in the dill, vinegar and a little pepper, and then add the yoghurt.

5 Chill, if time allows, then stir in the milk just before serving in soup bowls. Garnish with the reserved cucumber slices.

PREPARATION TIME:
15 MINUTES
PLUS CHILLING TIME

Curried Parsnip Soup

This recipe is equally good made with sweet potatoes or yams instead of parsnips.

SERVES 6	METRIC	IMPERIAL	AMERICAN
Parsnips, sliced	450 g	1 lb	1 lb
Onion, chopped	1	1	1
Butter or margarine	25 g	1 oz	2 tbsp
Curry powder	15 ml	1 tbsp	1 tbsp
Vegetable stock	600 ml	1 pt	2½ cups
Milk	300 ml	½ pt	1¼ cups
Salt and pepper			
Chopped parsley	15 ml	1 tbsp	1 tbsp
Hot Walnut Bread (page 147)			

1 Put the parsnips, onion and butter or margarine in a pan. Fry (sauté) gently, stirring, for 3 minutes.

2 Add the curry powder and fry for 1 minute.

3 Stir in the stock, bring to the boil, reduce the heat, cover and simmer for 15 minutes or until the parsnips are really tender.

4 Blend or purée in a food processor. Return to the pan.

5 Stir in the milk, season to taste and add the parsley. Heat through.

6 Serve ladled into soup bowls with hot walnut bread.

PREPARATION TIME:
10 MINUTES

COOKING TIME:
20 MINUTES

Golden Cheddar Soup

SERVES 4	METRIC	IMPERIAL	AMERICAN
Large potato, diced	1	1	1
Large onion, chopped	1	1	1
Carrot, chopped	1	1	1
Celery stick, chopped	1	1	1
Vegetable or chicken stock	600 ml	1 pt	2½ cups
Cheddar cheese, grated	100 g	4 oz	1 cup
Milk or single (light) cream	150 ml	¼ pt	⅔ cup
Chopped parsley	30 ml	2 tbsp	2 tbsp
Snipped chives, to garnish			

1 Simmer all the vegetables in the stock for 15 minutes or until soft.

2 Blend or purée in a food processor and return to the pan. Stir in the cheese, milk or cream and parsley. Heat through but do not boil.

3 Serve hot, garnished with chives.

PREPARATION TIME:
10 MINUTES

COOKING TIME:
15 MINUTES

Greek Egg and Lemon Soup

SERVES 6	METRIC	IMPERIAL	AMERICAN
Chicken or lamb stock	900 ml	1½ pts	3¾ cups
Long-grain rice	50 g	2 oz	¼ cup
Eggs	2	2	2
Small lemon	1	1	1
Water	15 ml	1 tbsp	1 tbsp
Salt and pepper			
Chopped parsley, to garnish			

1 Put the stock and rice in a pan. Bring to the boil and simmer for 10–12 minutes until the rice is cooked.

2 Break the eggs into a bowl. Squeeze in the juice from the lemon and add the water. Whisk to blend.

3 Whisk in one ladleful of the hot stock, then whisk in two more ladlefuls.

4 Remove the hot soup from the heat and stir in the egg mixture. Taste and season, if necessary.

5 Serve in soup bowls, garnished with chopped parsley.

PREPARATION TIME:
5 MINUTES

COOKING TIME:
12 MINUTES

Green Velvet Soup

SERVES 6	METRIC	IMPERIAL	AMERICAN
Spinach	450 g	1 lb	1 lb
Butter	15 g	½ oz	1 tbsp
Onion, chopped	1	1	1
Shelled fresh or frozen broad (lima) beans	175 g	6 oz	6 oz
Pinch of grated nutmeg			
Vegetable stock	600 ml	1 pt	2½ cups
Milk	300 ml	½ pt	1¼ cups
Salt and pepper			
Croûtons, to garnish			

1 Wash the spinach well, removing any thick stalks. Tear the leaves into pieces.

2 Melt the butter in a pan. Add the onion and fry (sauté) gently for 1 minute.

3 Add the spinach and stir until it cooks down a little.

4 Add the beans, nutmeg and stock. Bring to the boil, reduce the heat, cover and simmer for 15 minutes until the beans are soft.

5 Blend or purée in a food processor until smooth.

6 Return to the pan and add the milk. Season, if necessary. Reheat and serve in soup bowls, garnished with croûtons.

PREPARATION TIME: 10 MINUTES

COOKING TIME: 18 MINUTES

Mediterranean Summer Soup

SERVES 4	METRIC	IMPERIAL	AMERICAN
Slice of fresh bread	1	1	1
Oil	15 ml	1 tbsp	1 tbsp
Lemon juice	15 ml	1 tbsp	1 tbsp
Water	30 ml	2 tbsp	2 tbsp
Small onion, chopped	½	½	½
Small garlic clove	1	1	1
Red (bell) pepper, roughly diced	1	1	1
Cucumber, roughly chopped	½	½	½
Can of tomatoes	400 g	14 oz	1 large
Tomato purée (paste)	15 ml	1 tbsp	1 tbsp
Caster (superfine) sugar	5 ml	1 tsp	1 tsp
Salt and pepper			
Iced water	150 ml	¼ pt	⅔ cup
Chopped parsley, to garnish			

1 Break up the bread and place in a bowl with the oil, lemon juice and water. Leave to soak for 5 minutes.

2 Place in a blender or food processor with all the remaining ingredients except the iced water. Run the machine until smooth.

3 Stir in the iced water and re-season, if necessary.

4 Ladle into soup bowls and garnish with chopped parsley.

PREPARATION TIME:
10 MINUTES

Mushroom and Corn Chowder

SERVES 4	METRIC	IMPERIAL	AMERICAN
Button mushrooms, chopped	225 g	8 oz	8 oz
Onion, chopped	1	1	1
Butter or margarine	40 g	1½ oz	3 tbsp
Plain (all-purpose) flour	25 g	1 oz	¼ cup
Chicken stock	300 ml	½ pt	1¼ cups
Milk	300 ml	½ pt	1¼ cups
Can of sweetcorn (corn)	320 g	12 oz	1 large
Single (light) cream	30 ml	2 tbsp	2 tbsp
Salt and pepper			
Snipped chives, to garnish			

1 Fry (sauté) the mushrooms and onion gently in a pan with the butter or margarine for 3 minutes, stirring continually.

2 Add the flour and cook, stirring, for a further minute.

3 Remove from the heat and blend in the stock, milk and sweetcorn.

4 Return to the heat and bring to the boil, stirring. Reduce the heat and simmer gently for 10 minutes. Remove from the heat.

5 Season to taste and stir in the cream. Serve in soup bowls, garnished with chives.

PREPARATION TIME:
5 MINUTES

COOKING TIME:
14 MINUTES

Peanut Soup

SERVES 6	METRIC	IMPERIAL	AMERICAN
Small onion, chopped	1	1	1
Celery stick, chopped	1	1	1
Butter	25 g	1 oz	2 tbsp
Plain (all-purpose) flour	20 g	¾ oz	3 tbsp
Chicken stock	1 litre	1¾ pts	4¼ cups
Smooth peanut butter	225 g	8 oz	1 cup
Single (light) cream	200 ml	7 fl oz	scant 1 cup

Chopped peanuts and chopped parsley, to garnish

1 Fry (sauté) the onion and celery in the butter in a pan until softened but not browned.

2 Sprinkle in the flour and cook, stirring, for 1 minute.

3 Gradually blend in the stock, bring to the boil and simmer for 5 minutes.

4 Blend or purée in a food processor.

5 Return to the pan and blend in the peanut butter and cream. Reheat, but do not boil.

6 Serve in soup bowls garnished with chopped peanuts and parsley.

PREPARATION TIME: 5 MINUTES

COOKING TIME: 8–10 MINUTES

Quick Minestrone

If you have a food processor, use it to grate the vegetables.

SERVES 6	METRIC	IMPERIAL	AMERICAN
Small onion, grated	1	1	1
Oil	15 ml	1 tbsp	1 tbsp
Carrot, grated	1	1	1
Small parsnip or turnip, grated	1	1	1
Small cabbage, shredded	¼	¼	¼
Frozen peas	50 g	2 oz	2 oz
Quick-cook macaroni	25 g	1 oz	1 oz
Can of chopped tomatoes	400 g	14 oz	1 large
Vegetable stock cube	1	1	1
Dried oregano	2.5 ml	½ tsp	½ tsp
Salt and pepper			
Grated Parmesan cheese, to serve			

1 Fry (sauté) the onion in the oil in a large pan for 1 minute, stirring.

2 Add the remaining ingredients. Fill the tomato can with cold water and add to the pan. Add one further canful of water.

3 Bring to the boil, reduce the heat and simmer for 10 minutes or until the vegetables and pasta are soft.

4 Taste and re-season, if necessary.

5 Serve in soup bowls with Parmesan cheese to sprinkle over.

PREPARATION TIME:
10 MINUTES

COOKING TIME:
2 MINUTES

Watercress Soup

SERVES 6	METRIC	IMPERIAL	AMERICAN
Bunches of watercress	2	2	2
Onion, sliced	1	1	1
Large potato, diced	1	1	1
Butter or margarine	25 g	1 oz	2 tbsp
Chicken stock	600 ml	1 pt	2½ cups
Milk	300 ml	½ pt	1¼ cups
Salt and pepper			
Soured (dairy sour) cream or plain yoghurt, to garnish			

1 Wash the watercress, cut off and discard the feathery stalks and chop the leaves.

2 Place in a pan with the onion, potato and butter or margarine.

3 Cook, stirring, for 3 minutes.

4 Add the stock, bring to the boil, then reduce the heat, cover and simmer gently for 15–20 minutes until the vegetables are soft.

5 Blend or purée in a food processor.

6 Stir in the milk and season to taste.

7 Either reheat, without boiling, or chill. Serve in soup bowls, garnished with a spoonful of soured cream or yoghurt.

PREPARATION TIME:
10 MINUTES

COOKING TIME:
18–23 MINUTES

STARTERS

A sumptuous starter will set the scene for a truly memorable meal. It should be filling enough to stave off the first hunger pangs, but not so substantial as to dull the appetite for the main course. Remember to keep portions small and beautifully presented.

Asian Pears with Blue Cheese Mayonnaise

If not serving immediately, toss the fruit slices in lemon juice to prevent browning. If you can't buy Asian pears, ripe dessert pears are equally delicious.

SERVES 6	METRIC	IMPERIAL	AMERICAN
Danish Blue cheese	100 g	4 oz	4 oz
Mayonnaise	60 ml	4 tbsp	4 tbsp
Double (heavy) cream	45 ml	3 tbsp	3 tbsp
Lemon juice	5 ml	1 tsp	1 tsp
Black pepper			
Asian pears	4–6	4–6	4–6
Paprika and parsley sprigs, to garnish			

1 Crumble the cheese into a bowl and mash well with 15 ml/1 tbsp of the mayonnaise.

2 When fairly smooth, beat in the remainder of the mayonnaise, the cream and lemon juice. Add a good grinding of pepper.

3 Quarter, core and slice the pears, but do not peel.

4 Arrange the pear slices attractively on individual serving plates and spoon the mayonnaise to one side of the slices. Dust the mayonnaise with paprika and garnish each plate with a parsley sprig.

PREPARATION TIME:
10 MINUTES

Asparagus with Fresh Herb Hollandaise

SERVES 4	METRIC	IMPERIAL	AMERICAN
Asparagus	750 g	1½ lb	1½ lb
Bunch of watercress	1	1	1
Parsley sprigs	4	4	4
Marjoram leaves	8	8	8
Eggs	2	2	2
Lemon juice	30 ml	2 tbsp	2 tbsp
Butter, melted	100 g	4 oz	½ cup

1 Wash the asparagus. Trim off about 5 cm/2 in from the base of the stems. Tie the spears in a bundle.

2 Stand the bundle in a pan of lightly salted water. Cover with a lid (or foil if the pan is not deep enough).

3 Bring to the boil, reduce the heat and cook over a moderate heat for 10 minutes. Turn off the heat and leave for 5 minutes. Drain.

4 Meanwhile, cut off the watercress stalks. Wash the leaves and chop finely with the parsley and marjoram.

5 Whisk the eggs in a pan with the lemon juice, then gradually whisk in the melted butter. Cook over a gentle heat, whisking all the time until thickened. Do not boil. Stir in the watercress.

6 Lay the asparagus on warm plates, spoon a little sauce in a line over the stalks just below the heads. Serve straight away.

PREPARATION TIME:
15 MINUTES

COOKING TIME:
10 MINUTES

Aubergine Dip

SERVES 6	METRIC	IMPERIAL	AMERICAN
Large aubergine (eggplant)	1	1	1
Lemon juice	5 ml	1 tsp	1 tsp
Plain yoghurt	30 ml	2 tbsp	2 tbsp
Small onion, finely chopped	1	1	1
Low-fat soft cheese	175 g	6 oz	¾ cup
Snipped chives	5 ml	1 tsp	1 tsp
Salt and pepper			
French bread, to serve			

1 Cut the stalk off the aubergine and discard. Boil the aubergine in water for 10 minutes until tender, then drain.

2 Peel off the purple skin and sieve (strain) or blend the flesh with the lemon juice and yoghurt.

3 Beat in the onion, cheese and chives and season to taste.

4 Chill, if time allows, then serve with French bread.

PREPARATION TIME:
10 MINUTES
PLUS CHILLING TIME

Avocado South American-style

SERVES 4	METRIC	IMPERIAL	AMERICAN
Ripe avocados	2	2	2
Lemon juice	30 ml	2 tbsp	2 tbsp
Worcestershire sauce	30 ml	2 tbsp	2 tbsp
Small garlic clove, crushed	1	1	1
Chilli powder	1.5 ml	¼ tsp	¼ tsp
Olive oil	60 ml	4 tbsp	4 tbsp
Salt and pepper			
Piece of cucumber	5 cm	2 in	2 in
Tomatoes, chopped	2	2	2
Hot toast or tortilla chips, to serve			

1 Halve the avocados, remove the stones (pits) and scoop the flesh into a bowl.

2 Mash well with the lemon juice, then work in the Worcestershire sauce, garlic and chilli powder.

3 Add the oil, a little at a time, beating well after each addition.

4 Season to taste and stir in the cucumber and tomato.

5 Pile on to plates or into ramekins (custard cups) and serve with hot toast or tortilla chips.

PREPARATION TIME:
10 MINUTES

Brittany Artichokes

SERVES 4	METRIC	IMPERIAL	AMERICAN
Globe artichokes	4	4	4
Juice of 2 lemons			
Butter	50 g	2 oz	¼ cup
Soft cheese with garlic and herbs	100 g	4 oz	½ cup
Milk	60 ml	4 tbsp	4 tbsp

1 Twist off the artichoke stalks and trim the bases level so they will stand up. Trim off the points of the outer leaves with scissors, if preferred (this is not strictly necessary).

2 Cook in boiling water, to which the lemon juice has been added, for about 20 minutes or until a leaf pulls away easily. Drain and turn upside-down on kitchen paper for a few minutes. Transfer to serving plates.

3 Meanwhile, make the dipping sauce: melt the butter and cheese in a pan, stirring over a moderate heat. Gradually blend in the milk and heat through, stirring until smooth. Pour into four little individual dishes and serve with the artichokes.

4 To eat, pull off each leaf in turn, dip the base in the sauce and draw through the teeth to remove the fleshy part. When the hairy choke is revealed, cut or pull it off and eat the heart with a knife and fork and any remaining sauce.

PREPARATION TIME: 10 MINUTES

COOKING TIME: 20 MINUTES

Creamy Cucumber with Crab

Substitute prawns (shrimp) for crab, if you prefer. This recipe also makes a delicious light lunch or supper dish, served on a bed of plain boiled rice.

SERVES 4–6	METRIC	IMPERIAL	AMERICAN
Large cucumber, diced	1	1	1
Butter	50 g	2 oz	¼ cup
Button mushrooms, sliced	175 g	6 oz	6 oz
Plain (all-purpose) flour	10 ml	2 tsp	2 tsp
Chicken stock	150 ml	¼ pt	⅔ cup
Sherry	15 ml	1 tbsp	1 tbsp
Single (light) cream	90 ml	6 tbsp	6 tbsp
White crabmeat	100 g	4 oz	4 oz
Salt and pepper			
Chopped parsley, to garnish			
Hot Walnut Bread (page 147)			

1 Cook the cucumber in lightly salted, boiling water for 3 minutes. Drain, rinse with cold water and drain again.

2 Melt the butter in a pan, add the mushrooms and cook, stirring, for 2 minutes.

3 Add the cucumber, cover with a lid and cook gently for 2 minutes.

4 Blend in the flour, then gradually stir in the stock, sherry and cream until smooth.

5 Bring to the boil, stirring. Add the crabmeat and heat through.

6 Spoon into scallop shells or ramekins (custard cups), garnish with chopped parsley and serve with hot walnut bread or savoury wholemeal rolls.

<table>
<tr><td>PREPARATION TIME:
10 MINUTES</td><td></td><td>COOKING TIME:
10 MINUTES</td></tr>
</table>

Chinese-style Salad

This also makes a delicious summer lunch dish. Try it with canned tuna for a change.

SERVES 4–6	METRIC	IMPERIAL	AMERICAN
Bean sprouts	175 g	6 oz	6 oz
Red (bell) pepper, chopped	½	½	½
Peeled prawns (shrimp)	100 g	4 oz	4 oz
Soy sauce	10 ml	2 tsp	2 tsp
White vinegar	10 ml	2 tsp	2 tsp
Caster (superfine) sugar	5 ml	1 tsp	1 tsp
Olive or sesame oil	30 ml	2 tbsp	2 tbsp
Salt and pepper			
Lettuce leaves and chopped spring onion (scallion), to garnish			

1 Wash the bean sprouts and put in a bowl with the chopped pepper and prawns.

2 Blend together the remaining ingredients and pour over the bean sprouts. Toss well.

3 Pile on to lettuce leaves and garnish with a little chopped spring onion.

<table>
<tr><td>PREPARATION TIME:
5 MINUTES</td><td></td></tr>
</table>

Calamares a la Plancha

Contrary to popular belief, small squid, or calamares, are not chewy, but tender and full of flavour when cooked in this way.

SERVES 4	METRIC	IMPERIAL	AMERICAN
Onion, chopped	1	1	1
Garlic clove, finely chopped	2	2	2
Olive oil	60 ml	4 tbsp	4 tbsp
Small squid, cleaned and sliced into rings	450 g	1 lb	1 lb
Salt and pepper			
Chopped parsley	30 ml	2 tbsp	2 tbsp
Lemon wedges and crusty bread, to serve			

1 Gently fry (sauté) the onion and garlic in the oil for 2 minutes until softened but not browned.

2 Add the squid (including the tentacles) and toss gently until the rings turn pinkish-white.

3 Season with salt and pepper, cover the pan with a lid and cook over a very gentle heat for 5–10 minutes. The squid will now be bathed in lots of delicious juice.

4 Sprinkle with the chopped parsley, then spoon into warm shallow dishes and serve with plenty of lemon wedges to squeeze over and crusty bread to mop up the juices.

PREPARATION TIME:
5–10 MINUTES
PLUS CLEANING SQUID,
IF NECESSARY

COOKING TIME:
10–15 MINUTES

Garlicky Mushrooms

SERVES 4	METRIC	IMPERIAL	AMERICAN
Large, flat mushrooms	8	8	8
Butter	25 g	1 oz	2 tbsp
Large garlic clove, finely chopped	1	1	1
Salt and pepper			
Dry white wine	150 ml	¼ pt	⅔ cup
Single (light) cream or plain yoghurt	150 ml	¼ pt	⅔ cup
Chopped parsley, to garnish			
French bread, to serve			

1 Wash the mushrooms and pat dry on kitchen paper. Peel, if necessary.

2 Grease a large ovenproof dish with the butter.

3 Lay the mushrooms in the dish, stalks up.

4 Scatter the garlic over, season with a little salt and pepper, and pour over the wine and cream. Cover with foil.

5 Bake at 190°C/375°F/gas mark 5 for about 20 minutes until the mushrooms are tender.

6 Transfer the mushrooms to serving plates, spoon the sauce over and sprinkle with chopped parsley. Serve with French bread to mop up the juices.

PREPARATION TIME:
5 MINUTES

COOKING TIME:
20 MINUTES

Golden Camembert with Cranberry Sauce

This recipe is equally delicious with small portions of goats' cheese.

SERVES 6	METRIC	IMPERIAL	AMERICAN
Individual Camembert portions	6	6	6
Eggs, beaten	2	2	2
Fresh white breadcrumbs	50 g	2 oz	1 cup
Oil for deep-frying			
Salad, to garnish			
Cranberry sauce, to serve			

1 Dip the cheese portions in the egg, then the breadcrumbs. Repeat to coat thoroughly.

2 Heat the oil until a cube of day-old bread browns in 30 seconds. Fry (sauté) the cheeses for 2 minutes or until crisp and golden brown.

3 Drain on kitchen paper and transfer to serving plates. Add an attractive salad garnish and spoon a little cranberry sauce to the side of each cheese. Serve immediately.

PREPARATION TIME:
10 MINUTES

COOKING TIME:
2 MINUTES

Moorish Mushrooms

SERVES 4–6	METRIC	IMPERIAL	AMERICAN
Button mushrooms	450 g	1 lb	1 lb
Onion, chopped	1	1	1
Garlic clove, crushed	1	1	1
Olive oil	60 ml	4 tbsp	4 tbsp
Can of chopped tomatoes	400 g	14 oz	1 large
Caster (superfine) sugar	5 ml	1 tsp	1 tsp
Red wine	150 ml	¼ pt	⅔ cup
Salt and pepper			
Chopped parsley, to garnish			
Ciabatta or French bread, to serve			

1 Put the mushrooms, onion, garlic and oil in a pan and cook gently, stirring, for 3 minutes.

2 Add the tomatoes, sugar and wine. Bring to the boil, reduce the heat and simmer for 15 minutes or until the liquid is well reduced.

3 Season to taste and serve hot or chilled, sprinkled with chopped parsley, with ciabatta or French bread.

PREPARATION TIME:
5 MINUTES

COOKING TIME:
18 MINUTES

Melon and Clementine Cocktail

SERVES 6	METRIC	IMPERIAL	AMERICAN
Honeydew melon	1	1	1
Clementines	3	3	3
Pieces of stem ginger in syrup, finely chopped	2	2	2
Sherry	45 ml	3 tbsp	3 tbsp
Hot Walnut Bread (page 147), to serve			

1 Halve the melon, remove the seeds, then scoop out the flesh with a melon baller or cut into dice. Place in a bowl.

2 Peel and segment the clementines, discarding any pith. Add to the bowl.

3 Mix in the ginger, 30 ml/2 tbsp of the ginger syrup and the sherry. Toss well. Chill, if time allows, before serving in individual glass dishes with Hot Walnut Bread.

PREPARATION TIME: 10 MINUTES

Melon with Westphalian Ham

You can use any raw cured ham for this recipe, but Westphalian is usually a very good buy.

SERVES 4	METRIC	IMPERIAL	AMERICAN
Honeydew melon	1	1	1
Slices of Westphalian ham	4	4	4
Pickled gherkins (cornichons)	4	4	4
Pumpernickel, to serve			

1 Halve the melon, scoop out the seeds, cut each half into four wedges and peel them.

2 Halve each slice of ham lengthways and wrap each round a melon wedge.

3 Lay these on four individual serving plates.

4 Using a sharp knife, make four slices down each gherkin from the stalk end almost down to the base, then gently ease the slices apart to form a fan.

5 Lay one on each plate to garnish and serve with pumpernickel.

PREPARATION TIME:
5–10 MINUTES

Moules Marinières

SERVES 4–6	METRIC	IMPERIAL	AMERICAN
Mussels	1.75 kg	4 lb	4 lb
Butter	40 g	1½ oz	3 tbsp
Large onion, chopped	1	1	1
Wineglasses of dry white wine or vermouth	2	2	2
Wineglass of water	1	1	1
Black pepper			
Chopped parsley	30 ml	2 tbsp	2 tbsp
French bread, to serve			

1 Scrub the mussels and scrape off any beards and barnacles. Discard any that are damaged or do not close immediately when tapped. Rinse well in cold running water.

2 Heat the butter in a large pan. Fry (sauté) the onion gently for 1 minute without browning.

3 Add the mussels, wine or vermouth and water and a grinding of pepper. Bring to the boil, cover the pan and shake over a moderate heat for 5 minutes.

4 Discard any mussels that have not opened. Ladle into soup bowls with the liquor and sprinkle liberally with the chopped parsley.

5 Serve with lots of crusty French bread to mop up the juices.

PREPARATION TIME:
10–15 MINUTES

COOKING TIME:
6 MINUTES

Mushroom Pâté

SERVES 4	METRIC	IMPERIAL	AMERICAN
Butter or margarine	25 g	1 oz	2 tbsp
Small onion, finely chopped	1	1	1
Mushrooms, finely chopped	350 g	12 oz	12 oz
Lemon juice	15 ml	1 tbsp	1 tbsp
Low-fat soft cheese	225 g	8 oz	1 cup
Chopped parsley	30 ml	2 tbsp	2 tbsp
Hot buttered toast, to serve			

1 Melt the butter in a pan. Fry (sauté) the onion until pale golden.

2 Add the mushrooms and fry until no liquid remains, stirring all the time.

3 Add the lemon juice, turn into a bowl and allow to cool.

4 Beat in the cheese and parsley. Chill, if time allows, before serving with hot buttered toast.

PREPARATION TIME:
10 MINUTES
PLUS CHILLING TIME

COOKING TIME:
ABOUT 8 MINUTES

Pâté-stuffed Peppers

Choose (bell) peppers of an even size and shape for this recipe.

SERVES 6	METRIC	IMPERIAL	AMERICAN
Green pepper	1	1	1
Red or yellow pepper	1	1	1
Smooth liver pâté	225 g	8 oz	1 cup
Soft white breadcrumbs	25 g	1 oz	½ cup
Butter, melted	50 g	2 oz	¼ cup
Snipped chives	15 ml	1 tbsp	1 tbsp
Black pepper			
Salad, to garnish			

1 Cut the stalk ends off the peppers and remove the seeds.

2 Blend the pâté with the breadcrumbs, melted butter, herbs and a little black pepper until smooth.

3 Pack into the peppers, wrap in clingfilm (plastic wrap) and chill for at least 30 minutes until the filling is firm.

4 Cut each pepper into six slices, carefully transfer one of each colour to individual serving plates and garnish with a little salad before serving.

PREPARATION TIME:
5–10 MINUTES
PLUS CHILLING TIME

Pears with Creamy Tarragon Dressing

SERVES 6	METRIC	IMPERIAL	AMERICAN
Ripe pears	6	6	6
A few lettuce leaves			
Crème fraîche	150 ml	¼ pt	⅔ cup
Sunflower oil	30 ml	2 tbsp	2 tbsp
Lemon juice	10 ml	2 tsp	2 tsp
Chopped tarragon	30 ml	2 tbsp	2 tbsp
Caster (superfine) sugar	5 ml	1 tsp	1 tsp
Salt and pepper			
Small tarragon sprigs, to garnish			

1 Peel, halve and core the pears. Place cut side down on a bed of lettuce on individual serving plates.

2 Beat together the remaining ingredients and spoon over the pears. Chill, if time allows, before serving garnished with small tarragon sprigs.

PREPARATION TIME:
5–10 MINUTES
PLUS CHILLING TIME

Rosy Eggs

SERVES 4	METRIC	IMPERIAL	AMERICAN
Eggs, hard-boiled (hard-cooked)	4	4	4
Mayonnaise	15 ml	1 tbsp	1 tbsp
Tomato purée (paste)	10 ml	2 tsp	2 tsp
Salt and pepper			
Anchovy fillets	4	4	4
Stuffed olive, sliced	1	1	1
Lettuce and garlic bread, to serve			

1 Shell and halve the eggs, scoop out the yolks and place in a bowl.

2 Mash the yolks, then beat in the mayonnaise, tomato purée and salt and pepper to taste.

3 Pile back into the egg whites. Garnish each with a rolled anchovy fillet and a slice of stuffed olive.

4 Serve on a bed of lettuce with garlic bread.

PREPARATION TIME:
10 MINUTES
PLUS EGG COOKING TIME

Smoked Salmon Pâté

Ask for smoked salmon pieces at your local delicatessen.
They're much cheaper than slices.

SERVES 6	METRIC	IMPERIAL	AMERICAN
Smoked salmon pieces	225 g	8 oz	8 oz
Double (heavy) cream	150 ml	¼ pt	⅔ cup
Butter, softened	50 g	2 oz	¼ cup
Lemon juice	30 ml	2 tbsp	2 tbsp
Pinch of cayenne	1	1	1
Lemon wedges and parsley sprigs, to garnish			
Hot toast, to serve			

1 Discard any skin and bones from the salmon.

2 Turn on the blender or food processor and drop in the salmon pieces, a few at a time, with the cream.

3 Add the butter, a knob at a time, and blend until smooth.

4 Add the lemon juice and cayenne and run the machine briefly again. Chill, if time allows.

5 Spoon on to individual serving plates, garnish each with a lemon wedge and parsley sprig and serve with hot toast.

PREPARATION TIME:
5–10 MINUTES
PLUS CHILLING TIME

Sweet and Sour Runner Beans

Substitute half the quantity of whole French (green) beans if runner beans are not available.

SERVES 6	METRIC	IMPERIAL	AMERICAN
Runner beans	900 g	2 lb	2 lb
Streaky bacon rashers (slices), diced	6	6	6
Button mushrooms, sliced	100 g	4 oz	4 oz
Olive oil	30 ml	2 tbsp	2 tbsp
Worcestershire sauce	30 ml	2 tbsp	2 tbsp
Soy sauce	15 ml	1 tbsp	1 tbsp
Light brown sugar	30 ml	2 tbsp	2 tbsp
Wine vinegar	30 ml	2 tbsp	2 tbsp

1 String and slice the beans and cook in boiling, salted water for about 5 minutes until just tender. Drain.

2 In a large pan, quickly fry (sauté) the bacon and mushrooms in the oil until golden. Remove from the pan with a draining spoon.

3 Add the remaining ingredients to the juices in the pan. Stir until the sugar dissolves, then bring to the boil.

4 Add the bacon, mushrooms and beans. Toss over a gentle heat until heated through.

5 Serve straight away.

PREPARATION TIME: 15 MINUTES

COOKING TIME: 8–10 MINUTES

Tangy Whiting Goujons

SERVES 6	METRIC	IMPERIAL	AMERICAN
Whiting fillets, skinned	750 g	1½ lb	1½ lb
Plain (all-purpose) flour	25 g	1 oz	¼ cup
Salt and pepper			
Eggs, beaten	2	2	2
Fresh breadcrumbs	175 g	6 oz	3 cups
Mayonnaise	150 ml	¼ pt	⅔ cup
Grated rind and juice of 1 lime			
Oil for deep-frying			
Lime wedges, to garnish			

1 Cut the fish into strips, discarding any bones. Toss in the flour seasoned with salt and pepper.

2 Coat in the beaten egg, then the breadcrumbs.

3 Reserve a pinch of lime rind for garnish, then blend the mayonnaise with the remaining lime rind and the juice. Spoon into a small pot and sprinkle with the reserved lime rind.

4 Heat the oil until a cube of day-old bread browns in 30 seconds and deep-fry the fish for 4 minutes until golden.

5 Drain on kitchen paper, arrange on a dish around the pot of mayonnaise and garnish with lime wedges.

PREPARATION TIME:
15 MINUTES

COOKING TIME:
4 MINUTES

FISH

Fish is by nature comparatively quick to cook, which makes it ideal for inclusion in this book. Many of the recipes in this section would also make good starters, served in smaller portions.

Fish Creole

SERVES 4	METRIC	IMPERIAL	AMERICAN
Small white fish fillets, skinned	4	4	4
Plain (all-purpose) flour	30 ml	2 tbsp	2 tbsp
Salt and pepper			
Chilli powder	2.5 ml	½ tsp	½ tsp
Butter	25 g	1 oz	2 tbsp
Oil	30 ml	2 tbsp	2 tbsp
Bananas, halved	2	2	2
Lime or lemon wedges, to garnish			
Wild rice and green salad, to serve			

1 Dust the fish with the flour seasoned with a little salt and pepper and the chilli powder.

2 Melt half the butter and oil in a frying pan (skillet) and fry (sauté) the fish for 3 minutes on each side until lightly golden and cooked through.

3 Transfer to a warm serving dish and keep warm.

4 Fry the bananas in the remaining butter and oil for about 2 minutes until softening. Transfer to the serving dish. Garnish with lime or lemon wedges and serve hot with wild rice and a green salad.

PREPARATION TIME:
5 MINUTES

COOKING TIME:
8 MINUTES

Buttery Mackerel

SERVES 4	METRIC	IMPERIAL	AMERICAN
Whole mackerel, cleaned	4	4	4
Salt and pepper			
Butter	65 g	2½ oz	good ¼ cup
Oil	15 ml	1 tbsp	1 tbsp
Made English mustard	10 ml	2 tsp	2 tsp
Caster (superfine) sugar	2.5 ml	½ tsp	½ tsp
Lemon juice	5 ml	1 tsp	1 tsp
Parsley sprigs, to garnish			
New potatoes and broad (lima) beans, to serve			

1 Cut the heads off the mackerel, if you prefer, wipe inside and out with kitchen paper. Slash the fish in several places along each side with a sharp knife and season with salt and pepper.

2 Heat 15 g/½ oz/1 tbsp of the butter with the oil in a large frying pan (skillet).

3 Add the fish and fry (sauté) for about 5 minutes on each side until browned and cooked through.

4 Meanwhile, beat the remaining butter with the mustard, sugar, a little salt and pepper and the lemon juice. Shape into four neat pieces.

5 Remove the fish from the pan, drain on kitchen paper and transfer to warm serving plates.

6 Top each fish with a piece of the mustard butter and garnish with parsley. Serve with new potatoes and broad beans.

PREPARATION TIME:
10 MINUTES

COOKING TIME:
10 MINUTES

Swordfish or Tuna Steaks Peasant-style

SERVES 4	METRIC	IMPERIAL	AMERICAN
Swordfish or tuna steaks, skinned	4	4	4
Olive oil	15 ml	1 tbsp	1 tbsp
Butter	15 g	½ oz	1 tbsp
Garlic clove, chopped	1	1	1
Chopped parsley	15 ml	1 tbsp	1 tbsp
Salt and pepper			
Lemon wedges, to garnish			
Sautéed potatoes and French (green) beans, to serve			

1 Fry (sauté) the fish in the oil and butter for 5 minutes on one side until golden.

2 Turn over and sprinkle with the garlic and parsley, a good grinding of pepper and a little salt. Cover with foil or a lid and continue cooking for 5 minutes or until cooked through.

3 Garnish with lemon wedges. Serve with sautéed potatoes and French beans.

PREPARATION TIME:
5 MINUTES

COOKING TIME:
ABOUT 10 MINUTES

Fish and Potato Fry

SERVES 4	METRIC	IMPERIAL	AMERICAN
Butter or margarine	15 g	½ oz	1 tbsp
Oil	15 ml	1 tbsp	1 tbsp
Potatoes, grated	450 g	1 lb	1 lb
Salt and pepper			
White fish fillet, skinned and cubed	450 g	1 lb	1 lb
Passata (sieved tomatoes)	400 ml	14 fl oz	scant ¾ cup
Tomato purée (paste)	15 ml	1 tbsp	1 tbsp
Granulated sugar	5 ml	1 tsp	1 tsp
Peas, to serve			

1 Melt the butter or margarine and oil in a frying pan (skillet).

2 Add half the grated potato and press down well. Season.

3 Add the fish in a layer, then top with the remaining potato, press down and season.

4 Cover with a lid or foil and cook gently for 30 minutes until cooked through.

5 Meanwhile, heat the passata in a pan with the tomato purée, sugar and a little pepper.

6 Turn out the fish and potato fry on to a warm serving plate. Serve cut into wedges with the tomato sauce and peas.

PREPARATION TIME:
10 MINUTES

COOKING TIME:
30 MINUTES

Hearty Fish Stew

SERVES 4	METRIC	IMPERIAL	AMERICAN
Onion, thinly sliced	1	1	1
Carrots, thinly sliced	1	1	1
Large potatoes, diced	2	2	2
Large parsnip, diced	1	1	1
Small cabbage, shredded	¼	¼	¼
Butter or margarine	25 g	1 oz	2 tbsp
Can of chopped tomatoes	400 g	14 oz	1 large
Water	300 ml	½ pt	1¼ cups
Anchovy essence (extract)	5 ml	1 tsp	1 tsp
White fish, skinned and cubed	350 g	12 oz	12 oz
Salt and pepper			
Chopped parsley, to garnish			
Crusty bread, to serve			

1 Place the prepared vegetables in a large pan with the butter or margarine. Fry (sauté) over a gentle heat, stirring occasionally, for 5 minutes.

2 Add the tomatoes, water and anchovy essence. Bring to the boil, reduce the heat, cover and simmer for 15 minutes.

3 Add the fish and simmer for a further 5 minutes or until cooked.

4 Season to taste, then spoon into warm bowls, sprinkle with chopped parsley and serve with crusty bread.

PREPARATION TIME:
10–15 MINUTES

COOKING TIME:
25 MINUTES

Quick Kedgeree

SERVES 4	METRIC	IMPERIAL	AMERICAN
Long-grain rice	225 g	8 oz	1 cup
Turmeric	5 ml	1 tsp	1 tsp
Smoked fish fillet, such as haddock or cod	225 g	8 oz	8 oz
Hard-boiled (hard-cooked) eggs, roughly chopped	3	3	3
Chopped parsley	30 ml	2 tbsp	2 tbsp
Salt and pepper			
Pinch of grated nutmeg	1	1	1
Single (light) cream or evaporated milk	45 ml	3 tbsp	3 tbsp
Chopped parsley, to garnish			
Tomato salad, to serve			

1 Cook the rice in lightly salted boiling water to which the turmeric has been added for 10 minutes or until just cooked. Drain and return to the saucepan.

2 Meanwhile skin the fish and poach in water for 5–10 minutes until it flakes easily with a fork. Drain.

3 Break up the fish, discarding any bones. Add to the rice with the eggs, parsley, seasoning and nutmeg.

4 Stir in the cream or evaporated milk and heat through.

5 Garnish with chopped parsley. Serve with a tomato salad.

PREPARATION TIME: 10 MINUTES

COOKING TIME: 12 MINUTES

Saucy Smoked Mackerel

SERVES 4	METRIC	IMPERIAL	AMERICAN
Butter or margarine	40 g	1½ oz	3 tbsp
Plain (all-purpose) flour	20 g	¾ oz	3 tbsp
Milk	300 ml	½ pt	1¼ cups
Grated rind and juice of ½ lemon			
Horseradish relish	15 ml	1 tbsp	1 tbsp
Salt and pepper			
Lemon wedges and parsley sprigs, to garnish			
Plain boiled potatoes and green beans, to serve			

1 To make the sauce, put half the butter or margarine in a saucepan with the flour and milk. Bring to the boil, whisking all the time until smooth.

2 Stir in the lemon rind, horseradish and seasoning to taste. Cover with a circle of wet greaseproof (waxed) paper to prevent a skin forming.

3 Put the mackerel fillets on a grill (broiler) pan. Dot with the remaining butter and drizzle with lemon juice. Grill (broil) for 3–5 minutes on each side, basting occasionally with the pan juices, until cooked through.

4 Transfer to a warmed serving dish and keep warm.

5 Strain the juices and add to the sauce. Heat through. Spoon over the fish, garnish with lemon wedges and parsley sprigs. Serve hot with plain boiled potatoes and green beans.

PREPARATION TIME:
5–10 MINUTES

COOKING TIME:
10–15 MINUTES

Trout in Soured Cream

Use plain yoghurt instead of cream, if you prefer.

SERVES 4	METRIC	IMPERIAL	AMERICAN
Trout, cleaned	4	4	4
Salt and pepper			
Butter	15 g	½ oz	1 tbsp
Oil	15 ml	1 tbsp	1 tbsp
Soured (dairy sour) cream	150 ml	¼ pt	⅔ cup
Snipped chives	15 ml	1 tbsp	1 tbsp
Chopped parsley			
Toasted flaked (slivered) almonds, to garnish			
New potatoes and baby carrots, to serve			

1 Rinse the fish under running water. Pat dry on kitchen paper. Season and remove the heads, if preferred.

2 Heat the butter and oil in a large frying pan (skillet) and fry (sauté) the fish for 3 minutes on each side to brown.

3 Add the soured cream, herbs and a little more seasoning, if liked. Cover with foil or a lid and simmer for 6–8 minutes until the fish is cooked through.

4 Transfer the fish to warm serving plates. Stir the juices and cream together well and spoon over. Sprinkle with toasted almonds and serve hot with new potatoes and baby carrots.

PREPARATION TIME:
5 MINUTES

COOKING TIME:
12–20 MINUTES

Baked Stuffed Plaice

Use a food processor, if liked, to make the stuffing. Just add the ingredients one by one to the bowl while running the machine.

SERVES 4	METRIC	IMPERIAL	AMERICAN
Button mushrooms, finely chopped	100 g	4 oz	4 oz
Butter	25 g	1 oz	2 tbsp
Fresh breadcrumbs	50 g	2 oz	1 cup
Chopped parsley	15 ml	1 tbsp	1 tbsp
Salt and pepper			
Plaice fillets	4	4	4
Single (light) cream	150 ml	¼ pt	⅔ cup
Parsley sprigs, to garnish			
Sautéed potatoes and broccoli, to serve			

1 Fry (sauté) the mushrooms in the butter for 2 minutes, stirring. Add the breadcrumbs, parsley and a little salt and pepper.

2 Remove any dark skin from the plaice fillets (do not worry about white-skinned ones). Cut the fillets in half lengthways.

3 Divide the stuffing between the fillets. Fold over into three to encase the filling. Transfer to four individual ovenproof dishes. Spoon the cream over. Cover with foil.

4 Bake in the oven at 180°C/350°F/gas mark 4 for 20 minutes until cooked through. Garnish with parsley. Serve with sautéed potatoes and broccoli.

PREPARATION TIME:
10 MINUTES

COOKING TIME:
20 MINUTES

Salmon Parcels

SERVES 4	METRIC	IMPERIAL	AMERICAN
Small salmon steaks	4	4	4
Filo pastry (paste) sheets	4	4	4
Melted butter for brushing			
Tomatoes, skinned	2	2	2
Mushrooms, chopped	2	2	2
Dried mixed herbs	1.5 ml	¼ tsp	¼ tsp
Quick Hollandaise sauce:			
Eggs	2	2	2
Lemon juice	30 ml	2 tbsp	2 tbsp
Pinch of cayenne	1	1	1
Butter, melted	100 g	4 oz	½ cup
Salt and pepper			
Parsley springs, to garnish			
New potatoes and mangetout (snow peas), to serve			

1 Remove any skin and bones from the fish.

2 Brush the pastry sheets with a very little melted butter, fold in half and brush again.

3 Put a salmon steak in the centre of each piece of pastry. Mix the tomatoes and mushrooms with the herbs and spoon on top.

4 Draw up the pastry over the filling and squeeze together to form a pouch.

5 Transfer to a lightly buttered baking sheet and brush with the remaining butter. Bake in the oven at 200°C/400°F/gas mark 6 for about 10–15 minutes until golden.

6 To make the sauce, whisk the eggs in a small pan with the lemon juice and cayenne. Gradually whisk in the butter, then cook over a gentle heat, whisking all the time, until the mixture thickens. Do not boil. Taste and season, if necessary.

7 Transfer the salmon parcels to warm serving plates. spoon a little sauce to one side, garnish with parsley and serve with new potatoes and mangetout.

PREPARATION TIME:
15–20 MINUTES

COOKING TIME:
10–15 MINUTES

Cod Provençale

SERVES 4	METRIC	IMPERIAL	AMERICAN
Olive oil	15 ml	1 tbsp	1 tbsp
Onion, chopped	1	1	1
Garlic cloves, crushed	1–2	1–2	1–2
Red (bell) pepper, sliced	1	1	1
Can of chopped tomatoes	400 g	14 oz	1 large
Tomato purée (paste)	15 ml	1 tbsp	1 tbsp
Cod fillet, skinned and cubed	450 g	1 lb	1 lb
Salt and pepper			
Chopped parsley and a few black olives, to garnish			
Plain boiled rice and mixed salad, to serve			

1 Put the oil in a pan with onion and garlic and cook, stirring, for 2 minutes until softened but not browned.

2 Add the red pepper and fry (sauté) for 1 minute.

3 Stir in the tomatoes and purée, bring to the boil and boil rapidly for 5 minutes, stirring occasionally.

4 Add the cod and cook gently for 3–5 minutes until the fish is cooked but not breaking up.

5 Season to taste and serve garnished with chopped parsley and black olives on a bed of boiled rice, with a mixed salad.

PREPARATION TIME: 10 MINUTES COOKING TIME: 10–12 MINUTES

Whiting with Cheese and Anchovies

SERVES 4	METRIC	IMPERIAL	AMERICAN
Whiting fillets	4	4	4
Butter or margarine	15 g	½ oz	1 tbsp
Oil	10 ml	2 tsp	2 tsp
Tomatoes, sliced	2	2	2
Gruyère or Emmental (Swiss) cheese slices	4	4	4
Canned anchovy fillets, drained	8	8	8
Watercress, to garnish			
Buttered noodles and fried (sautéed) mushrooms, to serve			

1 Skin the fillets and remove any bones.

2 Heat the butter or margarine and oil in a large frying pan (skillet). Add the fish and fry for 2 minutes.

3 Top with the tomato slices, then the cheese, then arrange two anchovy fillets in a cross on top of each fish fillet.

4 Cover with a lid or foil and cook for 5–8 minutes until the fish is cooked and the cheese has melted.

5 Transfer to warm serving plates. Garnish with watercress and serve with buttered noodles and mushrooms.

PREPARATION TIME: 5 MINUTES

COOKING TIME: 7–10 MINUTES

Tandoori Fish

This also makes a delicious starter for eight people.

SERVES 4	METRIC	IMPERIAL	AMERICAN
White fish fillet	450 g	1 lb	1 lb
Plain yoghurt	150 ml	¼ pt	⅔ cup
Lemon juice	15 ml	1 tbsp	1 tbsp
Ground cumin	5 ml	1 tsp	1 tsp
Chilli powder	2.5 ml	½ tsp	½ tsp
Turmeric	2.5 ml	½ tsp	½ tsp
Salt			
Long-grain rice	175 g	6 oz	¾ cup
Can of chopped tomatoes	400 g	14 oz	1 large
Water	300 ml	½ pt	1¼ cups
Chopped coriander (cilantro) leaves	15 ml	1 tbsp	1 tbsp

Lemon wedges and coriander leaves, to garnish

1 Cut the fish into four equal pieces, discarding the skin and any bones. Lay in a shallow ovenproof dish just large enough to take the fish in a single layer.

2 Mix together the yoghurt, lemon juice, spices and a good pinch of salt. Spoon over the fish and turn the fish in the mixture to coat completely.

3 Leave to marinate for up to 3 hours, if time allows. If not, cook immediately in the oven at 180°C/350°F/ gas mark 4 for 20 minutes, basting occasionally.

4 Meanwhile, put the rice in a pan with the tomatoes and water. Bring to the boil, cover, reduce the heat and simmer for 20 minutes until cooked and the rice has absorbed the liquid. Add the chopped coriander and fork through.

5 Serve the fish with the rice, garnished with lemon wedges and fresh coriander leaves.

PREPARATION TIME:
10 MINUTES
PLUS MARINATING TIME

COOKING TIME:
20 MINUTES

BEEF

Except for mince, for quick-cooking you need to use the more expensive cuts. But the saving on fuel and the lack of waste make them a better buy than you would think …

And they taste fantastic!

Beef and Noodle Stir-fry

SERVES 4	METRIC	IMPERIAL	AMERICAN
Quick-cook Chinese egg noodles	100 g	4 oz	4 oz
Fillet or tenderised minute steak	225 g	8 oz	8 oz
Oil	30 ml	2 tbsp	2 tbsp
Onion, sliced	1	1	1
Carrot, cut into matchsticks	1	1	1
Celery stick, cut into matchsticks	1	1	1
Red (bell) pepper, cut into strips	1	1	1
Mushrooms, sliced	50 g	2 oz	2 oz
Cucumber, cut into matchsticks	¼	¼	¼
Sherry	30 ml	2 tbsp	2 tbsp
Soy sauce	30 ml	2 tbsp	2 tbsp
Light brown sugar	15 ml	1 tbsp	1 tbsp
Ground ginger	5 ml	1 tsp	1 tsp
Salt and pepper			

1 Cook the noodles according to the packet directions. Drain. Cut the steak diagonally into thin strips.

2 Heat the oil in a large frying pan (skillet) or wok. Add the steak and fry (sauté) for 2 minutes, stirring.

3 Add the onion, carrot and celery and fry for 3 minutes. Add the red pepper, mushrooms and cucumber and continue cooking, stirring, for 2 minutes.

4 Add the noodles and the remaining ingredients. Toss well until heated through. Serve straight away.

PREPARATION TIME:
10–15 MINUTES

COOKING TIME:
8–10 MINUTES

Burgundy-style Steak

SERVES 4	METRIC	IMPERIAL	AMERICAN
Butter	25 g	1 oz	2 tbsp
Olive oil	30 ml	2 tbsp	2 tbsp
Onion, sliced	1	1	1
Button mushrooms	100 g	4 oz	4 oz
Streaky bacon rashers (slices), diced	2	2	2
Fillet or rump steak, cubed	450 g	1 lb	1 lb
Cornflour (cornstarch)	15 ml	1 tbsp	1 tbsp
Dried mixed herbs	2.5 ml	½ tsp	½ tsp
Brandy	15 ml	1 tbsp	1 tbsp
Red wine	150 ml	¼ pt	⅔ cup
Beef stock	150 ml	¼ pt	⅔ cup
Salt and pepper			
Plain boiled rice and French (green) beans, to serve			

1 Melt half the butter and oil and fry (sauté) the onion, mushrooms and bacon for 3 minutes until soft and golden. Remove from the pan.

2 Toss the meat in the cornflour and herbs. Heat the remaining butter and oil in the pan and fry the meat for 5 minutes until browned and cooked.

3 Add the brandy and set alight. When the flames subside, add the mushroom mixture, wine and stock. Bring to the boil, stirring continually. Season to taste.

4 Serve with rice and green beans.

PREPARATION TIME: 5–10 MINUTES

COOKING TIME: 8–10 MINUTES

Pâté Steaks with Wine

SERVES 4	METRIC	IMPERIAL	AMERICAN
Thin slices of French stick	4	4	4
Butter	40 g	1½ oz	3 tbsp
Smooth liver pâté	50 g	2 oz	2 oz
Fillet steaks	4	4	4
Red wine	90 ml	6 tbsp	6 tbsp
Tomato purée (paste)	15 ml	1 tbsp	1 tbsp
Caster (superfine) sugar	2.5 ml	½ tsp	½ tsp
Dried marjoram	2.5 ml	½ tsp	½ tsp
Salt and pepper			
Parsley sprigs, to garnish			
Sautéed potatoes and green salad, to serve			

1 Spread the bread on both sides with a little of the butter. Fry (sauté) on each side until golden. Spread with the pâté and set aside.

2 Melt the remaining butter and fry the steaks for 2–3 minutes on each side for rare, 5–6 minutes each side for well done (depending on thickness).

3 Place a steak on each slice of bread and pâté on warm serving plates and keep warm.

4 Stir the wine, tomato purée, sugar and marjoram together in a pan. Bring to the boil, stirring, and season to taste.

5 Spoon the sauce over the steaks. Garnish with parsley and serve with sautéed potatoes and a salad.

PREPARATION TIME:
5 MINUTES

COOKING TIME:
UP TO 15 MINUTES

Minute Steak Diane

	METRIC	IMPERIAL	AMERICAN
Tenderised minute steaks OR well-beaten top rump steaks	4	4	4
Lemon juice	10 ml	2 tsp	2 tsp
Butter	25 g	1 oz	2 tbsp
Oil	15 ml	1 tbsp	1 tbsp
Small onion, grated	½	½	½
Chopped parsley	10 ml	2 tsp	2 tsp
Worcestershire sauce	30 ml	2 tbsp	2 tbsp
A few cherry tomatoes, sliced, to garnish			
Puréed potatoes and broccoli, to serve			

1 Brush the surfaces of the steaks with lemon juice.

2 Heat the butter and oil in a frying pan (skillet) and fry (sauté) the steaks for 2–3 minutes on each side until cooked through (do not attempt to cook them rare). Transfer to warm serving plates and keep warm.

3 Add the onion, parsley and Worcestershire sauce to the pan juices. Cook gently for 1 minute, then spoon over the steaks.

4 Garnish with tomato slices and serve with puréed potatoes and broccoli.

PREPARATION TIME:
5 MINUTES

COOKING TIME:
5–7 MINUTES

Pasta Grill

SERVES 4	METRIC	IMPERIAL	AMERICAN
Pasta shapes	225 g	8 oz	8 oz
Onion, chopped	1	1	1
Garlic clove, crushed	1	1	1
Minced (ground) beef	225 g	8 oz	2 cups
Can of tomatoes	400 g	14 oz	1 large
Dried mixed herbs	2.5 ml	½ tsp	½ tsp
Salt and pepper			
Cheddar cheese, grated	75 g	3 oz	¾ cup
Mixed salad, to serve			

1 Cook the pasta according to the packet directions. Drain.

2 Meanwhile, fry (sauté) the onion, garlic and beef in a pan and stir until browned and the meat grains are separate.

3 Add the tomatoes and break them up with a wooden spoon. Stir in the herbs and a little salt and pepper. Bring to the boil, reduce the heat and simmer for 10 minutes until cooked through and the sauce is reduced.

4 Stir in the pasta. Turn into a 1.5 litre/2½ pt/6 cup flameproof dish. Sprinkle with the cheese and place under a hot grill (broiler) until the cheese is melted and golden.

5 Serve hot with a mixed salad.

PREPARATION TIME:
5 MINUTES

COOKING TIME:
15 MINUTES

Pied-à-terre Pie

SERVES 4	METRIC	IMPERIAL	AMERICAN
Onion, finely chopped	1	1	1
Minced (ground) beef	450 g	1 lb	4 cups
Plain (all-purpose) flour	15 ml	1 tbsp	1 tbsp
Beef stock	300 ml	½ pt	1¼ cups
Gravy block or browning	5 ml	1 tsp	1 tsp
Frozen peas	75 g	3 oz	3 oz
Salt and pepper			
Potatoes, thinly sliced	450 g	1 lb	1 lb
Cheddar cheese, grated	75 g	3 oz	¾ cup
Carrots, to serve			

1 Fry (sauté) the onion and beef in a pan, stirring to break up the meat, until the meat is browned and the onion is softened.

2 Add the flour and cook for 1 minute.

3 Pour in the stock, gravy block or browning and add the peas. Bring to the boil, stirring. Reduce the heat, season to taste, and simmer for 10 minutes.

4 Meanwhile, cook the potato slices in boiling, salted water for about 4 minutes until tender. Drain.

5 Taste the meat mixture, re-season, if necessary, then turn into a 1.5 litre/2½ pt/6 cup flameproof dish.

6 Top with potato slices, then sprinkle with the grated cheese. Place under a hot grill (broiler) until golden brown. Serve with carrots.

PREPARATION TIME: 10 MINUTES

COOKING TIME: ABOUT 20 MINUTES

Popovers

A great way to use up leftover roast beef, or other meat, and vegetables on Monday.

MAKES 8	METRIC	IMPERIAL	AMERICAN
Oil	30 ml	2 tbsp	2 tbsp
Plain (all-purpose) flour	50 g	2 oz	½ cup
Pinch of salt	1	1	1
Egg	1	1	1
Milk	75 ml	5 tbsp	5 tbsp
Water	75 ml	5 tbsp	5 tbsp
Roast beef, finely diced	45 ml	3 tbsp	3 tbsp
Cooked leftover vegetables, chopped	45 ml	3 tbsp	3 tbsp
Gravy and a green vegetable, to serve			

1 Put 5 ml/1 tsp oil into each of the eight sections of a bun tin (muffin pan). Place in the oven to heat at 230°C/450°F/gas mark 8.

2 Put the flour and salt in a bowl. Add the egg and half the milk and water and beat until smooth. Stir in the remaining milk and water.

3 Divide the meat and vegetables between the sections. Spoon the batter over and cook towards the top of the oven for 15–18 minutes until puffy and golden.

4 Serve hot with gravy and a green vegetable.

PREPARATION TIME:
15–18 MINUTES

COOKING TIME:
5–10 MINUTES

Sausages Romanov

SERVES 4	METRIC	IMPERIAL	AMERICAN
Beef sausages	450 g	1 lb	1 lb
Red wine vinegar	30 ml	2 tbsp	2 tbsp
Olive oil	30 ml	2 tbsp	2 tbsp
Butter	50 g	2 oz	¼ cup
Mushrooms, sliced	100 g	4 oz	4 oz
Leek, sliced	1	1	1
Plain (all-purpose) flour	25 g	1 oz	¼ cup
Can of chopped tomatoes	400 g	14 oz	1 large
Salt and pepper			
Fresh breadcrumbs	50 g	2 oz	1 cup
Peas and crusty bread, to serve			

1 Cut the sausages into bite-sized pieces. Toss in the vinegar and oil.

2 Melt 40 g/1½ oz/3 tbsp of the butter in a pan and fry (sauté) the sausages, mushrooms and leek, stirring, for 3 minutes. Cover and cook gently for a further 3–4 minutes until the vegetables are soft.

3 Stir in the flour and tomatoes. Bring to the boil and simmer for 5 minutes, stirring. Season.

4 Turn into a greased ovenproof dish. Top with the breadcrumbs and dot with the remaining butter.

5 Bake in the oven at 220°C/425°F/gas mark 7 for about 20 minutes until cooked through and the topping is golden.

6 Serve with peas and crusty bread.

PREPARATION TIME:
5–10 MINUTES

COOKING TIME:
30 MINUTES

Salt Beef and Potato Salad

This salad is also good with cubes of boiled gammon.

SERVES 4–6	METRIC	IMPERIAL	AMERICAN
Cooked salt beef, cubed	175 g	6 oz	1½ cups
Cooked potatoes, cut into chunks	750 g	1½ lb	1½ lb
Small red (bell) pepper, diced	1	1	1
Cucumber, diced	¼	¼	¼
Can of sweetcorn (corn), drained	198 g	7 oz	1 small
Olive oil	60 ml	4 tbsp	4 tbsp
Wine vinegar	30 ml	2 tbsp	2 tbsp
Dijon mustard	2.5 ml	½ tsp	½ tsp
Caster (superfine) sugar	2.5 ml	½ tsp	½ tsp
Salt and pepper			
Onion rings, to garnish			

1 Put the meat and vegetables in a large salad bowl.

2 Blend together the oil, vinegar, mustard, sugar and
a little salt and pepper and pour over the meat and
vegetables. Toss well.

3 Garnish with onion rings and serve.

PREPARATION TIME:
10 MINUTES

Quick Chilli

Serve with Cornmeal Pancakes (page 145) instead of rice, if you prefer.

SERVES 4	METRIC	IMPERIAL	AMERICAN
Onion, chopped	1	1	1
Garlic clove, crushed	1	1	1
Minced (ground) beef	350 g	12 oz	3 cups
Hot chilli powder	2.5 ml	½ tsp	½ tsp
Ground cumin	5 ml	1 tsp	1 tsp
Dried oregano	5 ml	1 tsp	1 tsp
Can of tomatoes	400 g	14 oz	1 large
Can of red kidney beans	425 g	15 oz	1 large
Tomato purée (paste)	15 ml	1 tbsp	1 tbsp
Salt and pepper			

Plain boiled rice, grated Cheddar cheese, and shredded lettuce, to serve

1 Put the onion, garlic and beef in a pan and fry (sauté) until browned and the grains of meat are separate.

2 Add the chilli powder and cumin and fry for 1 minute.

3 Stir in the oregano and tomatoes and break up with a wooden spoon, then add the beans, tomato purée and seasoning to taste.

4 Bring to the boil, reduce the heat and simmer for 10–15 minutes until reduced and a good rich colour.

5 Serve with plain boiled rice, with grated cheese and shredded lettuce to sprinkle over.

PREPARATION TIME:
5 MINUTES

COOKING TIME:
15–20 MINUTES

LAMB

*One of the most versatile of meats, lamb
lends itself to dishes from all over the world.*

Eastern Lamb

A great way of using up the leftover Sunday joint. Use any leftover vegetables and gravy with a little tomato purée (paste) and curry powder to taste to make a curry accompaniment.

SERVES 4	METRIC	IMPERIAL	AMERICAN
Onion, sliced	1	1	1
Oil	15 ml	1 tbsp	1 tbsp
Cooked lamb, diced	225 g	8 oz	2 cups
Garlic clove, crushed	1	1	1
Ground ginger	2.5 ml	½ tsp	½ tsp
Ground cumin	2.5 ml	½ tsp	½ tsp
Ground coriander (cilantro)	2.5 ml	½ tsp	½ tsp
Turmeric	7.5 ml	1½ tsp	1½ tsp
Plain yoghurt	150 ml	¼ pt	⅔ cup
Salt and pepper			
Desiccated (shredded) coconut and currants, to garnish			
Pilau rice, to serve			

1 Fry (sauté) the onion in the oil for 3 minutes until turning golden.

2 Add the lamb and the remaining ingredients. Simmer for about 20 minutes, stirring occasionally, until almost dry (the mixture will curdle and look watery at first).

3 Serve on a bed of pilau rice, with desiccated coconut and currants sprinkled over.

PREPARATION TIME:
5 MINUTES

COOKING TIME:
23 MINUTES

Greek-style Lamb Kebabs

These kebabs are equally delicious prepared with cubes of pork fillet.

SERVES 4	METRIC	IMPERIAL	AMERICAN
Lamb neck fillet	350 g	12 oz	12 oz
Olive oil	15 ml	1 tbsp	1 tbsp
Red wine vinegar	10 ml	2 tsp	2 tsp
Dried oregano	5 ml	1 tsp	1 tsp
Salt and pepper			
Small green (bell) pepper	1	1	1
Button mushrooms	8	8	8

Buttered rice and a mixed salad with olives and Feta cheese, to serve

1 Cut the meat into cubes. Put in a bowl.

2 Drizzle with the oil, vinegar, oregano and seasoning. Toss and leave for at least 10 minutes, longer if possible.

3 Cut the pepper into 12 pieces. Thread the meat on to four skewers, alternating with mushrooms and pepper pieces.

4 Grill (broil) for about 10 minutes until golden and cooked through, turning once or twice and brushing with any leftover marinade.

5 Serve hot with buttered rice and a mixed salad topped with olives and Feta cheese.

PREPARATION TIME:
5 MINUTES
PLUS MARINATING

COOKING TIME:
10 MINUTES

Lemon-glazed Cutlets

Try this with other citrus fruit too. For larger appetites, double the ingredients.

SERVES 4	METRIC	IMPERIAL	AMERICAN
Lamb cutlets	4	4	4
Plain (all-purpose) flour, seasoned	15 ml	1 tbsp	1 tbsp
Butter	25 g	1 oz	2 tbsp
Grated rind and juice of 1 lemon			
Caster (superfine) sugar	10 ml	2 tsp	2 tsp
Chopped parsley, to garnish			
Buttered noodles and matchstick carrots, to serve			

1 Coat the lamb cutlets in the seasoned flour, tapping off any excess.

2 Fry (sauté), turning once, in the butter for about 10 minutes until browned and cooked through.

3 Remove and keep warm.

4 Drain off all but 15 ml/1 tbsp of the fat from the pan. Add the lemon juice and rind and the sugar and heat through.

5 Spoon over the cutlets, garnish with parsley and serve immediately with buttered noodles and matchstick carrots.

PREPARATION TIME: 5 MINUTES COOKING TIME: 12 MINUTES

Liver and Bacon with Onion Sauce

For larger appetites, cook more slices of liver.

SERVES 4	METRIC	IMPERIAL	AMERICAN
Bacon rasher (slices)	8	8	8
Oil	15 ml	1 tbsp	1 tbsp
Slices of lambs' liver	4	4	4
Onions, roughly chopped	3	3	3
Water	150 ml	¼ pt	⅔ cup
Plain (all-purpose) flour	20 g	¾ oz	3 tbsp
Milk	150 ml	¼ pt	⅔ cup
Salt and pepper			
Chopped parsley, to garnish			
Plain boiled potatoes and a green vegetable, to serve			

1 Dry-fry the bacon in a frying pan (skillet) until browned on both sides. Transfer to a serving dish and keep warm.

2 Heat the oil in the same pan and fry (sauté) the liver for about 4 minutes, turning once, until browned and just cooked.

3 Meanwhile, boil the onions in the water in a covered pan for 4 minutes. Blend the flour and milk, add to the pan and boil for 2 minutes, stirring. Season to taste.

4 Garnish the liver and bacon with parsley and serve with the onion sauce, boiled potatoes and a green vegetable.

PREPARATION TIME:
5 MINUTES

COOKING TIME:
ABOUT 10 MINUTES

Quick Moussaka

Use minced (ground) beef instead of lamb, if you prefer.

SERVES 4	METRIC	IMPERIAL	AMERICAN
Onion, finely chopped	1	1	1
Garlic clove, crushed	1	1	1
Minced (ground) lamb	350 g	12 oz	3 cups
Lamb or chicken stock	150 ml	¼ pt	⅔ cup
Tomato purée (paste)	30 ml	2 tbsp	2 tbsp
Ground cinnamon	5 ml	1 tsp	1 tsp
Dried oregano	2.5 ml	½ tsp	½ tsp
Salt and pepper			
Aubergine (eggplant), sliced	1	1	1
Plain yoghurt	150 ml	¼ pt	⅔ cup
Egg	1	1	1
Cheddar cheese, grated	75 g	3 oz	¾ cup
Herby Pittas (page 146) and green salad, to serve			

1 Fry (sauté) the onion, garlic and mince together in a saucepan, stirring until the grains of meat are browned and separate.

2 Add the stock and boil for about 15 minutes until nearly all the liquid has evaporated.

3 Stir in the tomato purée, cinnamon and oregano. Season to taste and simmer for 5 minutes.

4 Meanwhile, boil the aubergine in salted water for about 5 minutes or until tender. Drain.

5 Layer the meat mixture and aubergine slices in a 1.5 litre/2½ pt/6 cup flameproof dish, finishing with a layer of aubergine.

6 Beat the yoghurt, egg and cheese together and spoon over. Place under a moderately hot grill (broiler) for about 5 minutes until the topping is set and golden.

7 Serve with Herby Pittas and a green salad.

PREPARATION TIME:
10 MINUTES

COOKING TIME:
ABOUT 20 MINUTES

Rosie's Cutlets

Try this dish with leg of lamb steaks, but remember they'll take a little longer to cook.

SERVES 4	METRIC	IMPERIAL	AMERICAN
Butter	25 g	1 oz	2 tbsp
Thin lamb cutlets	8	8	8
Garlic clove, crushed	1	1	1
Dried rosemary, crushed	5 ml	1 tsp	1 tsp
Water	60 ml	4 tbsp	4 tbsp
Salt and pepper			
Watercress, to garnish			
Sautéed potatoes and cauliflower cheese, to serve			

1 Melt the butter in a frying pan (skillet). Add the cutlets and brown on both sides.

2 Add the remaining ingredients, cover with foil or a lid and simmer for 10 minutes.

3 Transfer to a warm serving dish. Garnish with watercress and serve with sautéed potatoes and cauliflower cheese.

PREPARATION TIME:
5 MINUTES

COOKING TIME:
12 MINUTES

Saucy Lamb with Capers

SERVES 4	METRIC	IMPERIAL	AMERICAN
Butter or margarine	75 g	3 oz	⅓ cup
Slices of bread, cubed	3	3	3
Marrow (squash), peeled and diced	350 g	12 oz	12 oz
Mushrooms, quartered	100 g	4 oz	4 oz
Cooked lamb, diced	175 g	6 oz	1½ cups
Plain (all-purpose) flour	15 ml	1 tbsp	1 tbsp
Chicken or lamb stock	300 ml	½ pt	1¼ cups
Capers, chopped	15 ml	1 tbsp	1 tbsp
Chopped parsley	15 ml	1 tbsp	1 tbsp
Egg, beaten	1	1	1
Salt and pepper			
Shredded white cabbage in vinaigrette dressing, to serve			

1 Melt 50 g/2 oz /¼ cup of the butter or margarine in a pan. Toss the bread in it to coat, then remove from the pan and set aside.

2 Melt the remaining fat in the pan. Add the marrow and the mushrooms. Cover and cook gently for 5–10 minutes until the vegetables are tender, shaking the pan occasionally. Add the lamb and cook for 2 minutes.

3 Add the flour and cook, stirring, for 1 minute. Blend in the stock and add the capers. Bring to the boil and cook for 2 minutes, stirring.

4 Blend in the parsley and egg and season to taste.

5 Spoon into four individual flameproof dishes. Top with the bread and place under a hot grill (broiler) until the bread is browned. Serve hot with shredded cabbage in vinaigrette dressing.

PREPARATION TIME: 10 MINUTES

COOKING TIME: 10–15 MINUTES

Tiddly Kidneys

SERVES 4	METRIC	IMPERIAL	AMERICAN
Butter or margarine	25 g	1 oz	2 tbsp
Lambs' kidneys, cored and quartered	8	8	8
Mushrooms, sliced	100 g	4 oz	4 oz
Onions, sliced	2	2	2
Single (light) cream	45 ml	3 tbsp	3 tbsp
Sherry	15 ml	1 tbsp	1 tbsp
Salt and pepper			
Chopped parsley, to garnish			
Creamed potatoes and leaf spinach, to serve			

1 Melt the fat in a frying pan (skillet). Add the kidneys, mushrooms and onions. Cover with foil or a lid and cook, stirring occasionally, for 10 minutes.

2 Add the cream, sherry and seasoning. Heat through.

3 Spoon into a nest of creamed potatoes, sprinkle with chopped parsley and serve with leaf spinach.

PREPARATION TIME: 10 MINUTES

COOKING TIME: 10–12 MINUTES

Somerset Lamb

SERVES 4	METRIC	IMPERIAL	AMERICAN
Onion, thinly sliced	1	1	1
Cooking (tart) apple, sliced	1	1	1
Oil	15 ml	1 tbsp	1 tbsp
Lamb chump chops	4	4	4
Plain (all-purpose) flour	20 g	¾ oz	3 tbsp
Cider or apple juice	300 ml	½ pt	1¼ cups
Chopped mint	15 ml	1 tbsp	1 tbsp
Salt and pepper			
Mint sprigs, to garnish			
Jacket potatoes and spring greens (spring cabbage), to serve			

1 Fry (sauté) the onion and apple in the oil for 3–4 minutes until softened. Remove from the pan.

2 Trim any fat from the chops. Fry for about 10–15 minutes, turning once, until just cooked through. Return the onion and apple to the pan for the last 5 minutes.

3 Transfer the onion, apple and chops to a warm serving dish and keep warm.

4 Blend the flour with a little of the cider or apple juice. Stir in the remainder and pour into the pan. Add the mint, bring to the boil and cook for 2 minutes, stirring. Season to taste.

5 Spoon the sauce over the lamb, garnish with mint and serve with jacket potatoes and spring greens.

PREPARATION TIME:
10 MINUTES

COOKING TIME:
15–20 MINUTES

PORK

Pork is one of the richest and most flavoursome of meats but beware of cooking it to death, when it becomes dry and stringy. All these dishes will give you succulent, tender results. But don't keep prodding the pork with a fork as it cooks or all the juice will run out.

Bacon and Avocado Salad

SERVES 4	METRIC	IMPERIAL	AMERICAN
Eggs	4	4	4
Lemon juice	10 ml	2 tsp	2 tsp
Streaky bacon rashers (slices)	4	4	4
Avocados	2	2	2
Mixed salad leaves (including radiccio or lollo rosso)	225 g	8 oz	8 oz
Olive oil	30 ml	2 tbsp	2 tbsp
Wine vinegar	10 ml	2 tsp	2 tsp
Salt and pepper			
Onion rings and croûtons, to garnish			
Herby Pittas (page 146), to serve			

1 Poach the eggs in gently simmering water, to which half the lemon juice has been added, for about 3 minutes until the whites are set but the yolk is still soft (or longer if you like them hard).

2 Lift them out with a draining spoon and place in a bowl of cold water to prevent cooking any further.

3 Grill (broil) or dry-fry the bacon rashers until crisp. Cut into pieces with scissors.

4 Halve, peel and slice the avocados, discarding the stones (pits). Toss in the remaining lemon juice.

5 Put the salad leaves in a bowl, add the avocado and bacon and toss in the oil, vinegar and a little salt and pepper. Transfer to four individual serving bowls.

6 Lift the eggs out of the water with a draining spoon and put one in each bowl. Garnish with onion rings and croûtons and serve with Herby Pittas.

PREPARATION TIME:
10 MINUTES

COOKING TIME:
ABOUT 6 MINUTES

Barbecued Pork

SERVES 4	METRIC	IMPERIAL	AMERICAN
Butter or margarine	15 g	½ oz	1 tbsp
Pork shoulder steaks	4	4	4
Lemon juice	15 ml	1 tbsp	1 tbsp
Malt vinegar	15 ml	1 tbsp	1 tbsp
Tomato purée (paste)	30 ml	2 tbsp	2 tbsp
Worcestershire sauce	15 ml	1 tbsp	1 tbsp
Golden (light corn) syrup	30 ml	2 tbsp	2 tbsp

Savoury rice and watercress and bean sprout salad, to serve

1 Melt the butter or margarine in a large frying pan (skillet). Add the pork and fry (sauté) for 3 minutes on each side to brown.

2 Blend together the remaining ingredients. Spoon over the pork. Cook over a moderate heat for 10 minutes, turning occasionally, until glazed.

3 Serve on a bed of savoury rice with a watercress and bean sprout salad.

PREPARATION TIME:
5 MINUTES

COOKING TIME:
16 MINUTES

Austrian Pork Chops

SERVES 4	METRIC	IMPERIAL	AMERICAN
Boneless thin pork chops	4	4	4
Olive oil	15 ml	1 tbsp	1 tbsp
Onion, thinly sliced	1	1	1
Garlic clove, crushed	1	1	1
Small cabbage, shredded	½	½	½
Vegetable or pork stock	150 ml	¼ pt	⅔ cup
Caraway seeds	15 ml	1 tbsp	1 tbsp
Salt and pepper			
Chopped parsley, to garnish			
Boiled potatoes, to serve			

1 Fry (sauté) the chops in the oil in a deep frying pan (skillet) for 3 minutes on each side to brown. Remove from the pan.

2 Add the onion and garlic and fry for 2 minutes.

3 Stir in the cabbage and cook, stirring, for about 3 minutes until it softens slightly. Add the stock.

4 Lay the chops on top, sprinkle with caraway seeds and a little salt and pepper. Cover with foil or a lid, reduce the heat and simmer for 20 minutes until tender.

5 Garnish with chopped parsley and serve with plain boiled potatoes.

PREPARATION TIME:
10 MINUTES

COOKING TIME:
ABOUT 30 MINUTES

Broccoli and Ham Cheese

Omit the ham to turn this into a delicious accompaniment for plain grills or a vegetarian lunch dish, if you use vegetarian cheese.

SERVES 4	METRIC	IMPERIAL	AMERICAN
Broccoli	450 g	1 lb	1 lb
Slices of ham	4	4	4
Plain (all-purpose) flour	25 g	1 oz	¼ cup
Butter or margarine	25 g	1 oz	2 tbsp
Milk	300 g	½ pt	1¼ cups
Cheddar cheese, grated	100 g	4 oz	1 cup
Salt and pepper			
Crusty bread, to serve			

1 Separate the broccoli into florets and cook in boiling, salted water for about 5 minutes until tender.

2 Divide into eight bundles and wrap half a slice of ham around each.

3 Lay side-by-side in a buttered ovenproof dish.

4 Whisk the flour and butter or margarine into the milk in a pan. Bring to the boil and boil for 2 minutes, whisking all the time until thickened and smooth. Stir in 75 g/3 oz/¾ cup of the cheese and season to taste.

5 Pour the sauce over the broccoli and ham. Sprinkle with the remaining cheese and grill (broil) for about 4 minutes until golden brown. Serve with crusty bread.

PREPARATION TIME: 10 MINUTES

COOKING TIME: 10 MINUTES

Deluxe Grill

SERVES 4	METRIC	IMPERIAL	AMERICAN
Gammon steaks	4	4	4
Can of pineapple chunks, drained	200 g	7 oz	1 small
Tomatoes, skinned and chopped	4	4	4
Havarti, Gruyère or Emmental (Swiss) cheese slices	4	4	4
Watercress, to garnish			
Sautéed potatoes and French (green) beans, to serve			

1 Snip the edges of the gammon with scissors to prevent curling.

2 Roughly chop the pineapple and mix with the tomatoes.

3 Grill (broil) the gammon for 5 minutes on each side.

4 Spread the fruit over and top each with a slice of cheese.

5 Return to the grill (broiler) until the cheese has melted and the fruit is hot.

6 Garnish with watercress and serve with sautéed potatoes and French beans.

PREPARATION TIME:
10 MINUTES

COOKING TIME:
ABOUT 15 MINUTES

Devilled Kidneys

You can use lambs' kidneys instead, in which case use eight for four people.

SERVES 4	METRIC	IMPERIAL	AMERICAN
Pigs' kidneys	4	4	4
Streaky bacon rashers (slices)	4	4	4
Butter or margarine	50 g	2 oz	¼ cup
Mild curry powder	5 ml	1 tsp	1 tsp
Made English mustard	2.5 ml	½ tsp	½ tsp
Worcestershire sauce	10 ml	2 tsp	2 tsp
Tomato ketchup (catsup)	30 ml	2 tbsp	2 tbsp
Salt and pepper			
Chopped parsley, to garnish			
Plain boiled rice and courgettes (zucchini), to serve			

1 Cut the kidneys into bite-sized pieces, discarding the cores. Dice the bacon.

2 Melt the butter or margarine in a frying pan (skillet) and fry (sauté) the kidneys and bacon over a moderate heat for 3 minutes, stirring.

3 Add the remaining ingredients, mix well and cook, stirring, for about 5–8 minutes until the kidneys are cooked but still tender and bathed in sauce.

4 Garnish with parsley. Serve with rice and courgettes.

PREPARATION TIME: 5 MINUTES

COOKING TIME: 8–11 MINUTES

Fegatini

Use ripe tomatoes for the sauce for these meatballs.

SERVES 4	METRIC	IMPERIAL	AMERICAN
Pigs' liver	350 g	12 oz	12 oz
Onions	2	2	2
Slice of bread	1	1	1
Chopped sage	15 ml	1 tbsp	1 tbsp
Egg, beaten	1	1	1
Salt and pepper			
Olive oil	15 ml	1 tbsp	1 tbsp
Tomatoes, quartered	450 g	1 lb	1 lb
Tomato purée (paste)	15 ml	1 tbsp	1 tbsp
Water	60 ml	4 tbsp	4 tbsp
Sugar	2.5 ml	½ tsp	½ tsp

Tagliatelle and green salad, to serve

1 Coarsely mince (grind) or process the liver, one onion and the bread. Add the sage, egg and seasoning and mix well.

2 Chop the remaining onion. Heat the oil in a pan. Add the onion and cook gently for about 2 minutes until softened. Add the tomatoes, tomato purée and water, cover and cook for about 5 minutes, stirring occasionally, until pulpy. Season and add the sugar.

3 Meanwhile, bring a large pan of salted water to the boil. Drop in tablespoonfuls of the liver mixture and simmer for about 4 minutes until cooked through. Drain.

4 Put the cooked balls of liver mixture in the sauce, heat through and serve with tagliatelle and a salad.

PREPARATION TIME:
10 MINUTES

COOKING TIME:
ABOUT 10 MINUTES

Sticky Orange Steaks

SERVES 4	METRIC	IMPERIAL	AMERICAN
Pork or bacon steaks	4	4	4
Butter or margarine	15 g	½ oz	1 tbsp
Shredless orange marmalade	15 ml	1 tbsp	1 tbsp
Ground ginger	2.5 ml	½ tsp	½ tsp
Orange juice	5 ml	1 tsp	1 tsp
Orange slices, to garnish			
Buttered noodles and mangetout (snow peas), to serve			

1 Fry (sauté) the steaks on one side in the butter or margarine for 5 minutes.

2 Mix together the marmalade, ginger and orange juice. Turn the steaks over and brush with this mixture. Fry for a further 5 minutes, basting occasionally with the juices.

3 Place the pan under a hot grill (broiler) for 2 minutes until the glaze is sticky. Transfer the steaks to warm serving plates, garnish with orange slices and serve hot with buttered noodles and mangetout.

PREPARATION TIME:
2 MINUTES

COOKING TIME:
12 MINUTES

Oriental Pork Slices

SERVES 4	METRIC	IMPERIAL	AMERICAN
Belly pork slices	8	8	8
Cornflour (cornstarch)	10 ml	2 tsp	2 tsp
Vinegar	15 ml	1 tbsp	1 tbsp
Can of crushed pineapple	250 g	9 oz	1 small
Tomato ketchup (catsup)	30 ml	2 tbsp	2 tbsp
Soy sauce	15 ml	1 tbsp	1 tbsp
Cucumber, diced	¼	¼	¼

*Plain boiled rice and green (bell) pepper and grated carrot salad,
to serve*

1 Discard any rind or bones in the pork, then fry
(sauté) the slices over a moderate heat for about
15–20 minutes, turning once or twice, until browned
and cooked through.

2 Meanwhile, blend the cornflour with the vinegar in a
pan.

3 Add the remaining ingredients. Bring to the boil,
stirring, and simmer for 5 minutes, stirring
occasionally.

4 Spoon over the pork and serve with rice and a green
pepper and grated carrot salad.

PREPARATION TIME:
5 MINUTES

COOKING TIME:
20–25 MINUTES

Pork Stroganoff

This recipe is also good made with chicken breasts or fillet steak.

SERVES 4	METRIC	IMPERIAL	AMERICAN
Pork fillet	350 g	12 oz	12 oz
Butter or margarine	25 g	1 oz	2 tbsp
Onion, sliced	1	1	1
Mushrooms, sliced	100 g	4 oz	4 oz
Brandy	15 ml	1 tbsp	1 tbsp
Soured (dairy sour) cream	150 ml	¼ pt	⅔ cup
Salt and pepper			
Chopped parsley, to garnish			
Boiled rice tossed with a knob of butter and green salad, to serve			

1 Cut the pork into thin strips.

2 Melt the butter or margarine and fry (sauté) the onion and mushrooms for 3 minutes to soften.

3 Add the pork strips and fry for 5–8 minutes until cooked through.

4 Put the brandy in a soup ladle, set alight, then pour into the pan. Cook until the flames subside. Stir in the cream and heat through but do not boil.

5 Season to taste. Garnish with chopped parsley and serve with buttered rice and a green salad.

PREPARATION TIME:
10 MINUTES

COOKING TIME:
10–12 MINUTES

Spaghetti with Bacon and Eggs

Use less or more spaghetti according to appetites.

SERVES 4	METRIC	IMPERIAL	AMERICAN
Onion, finely chopped	1	1	1
Garlic cloves, crushed	2	2	2
Streaky bacon rashers (slices), diced	6	6	6
Olive oil	60 ml	4 tbsp	4 tbsp
Spaghetti	350 g	12 oz	12 oz
Chopped parsley	15 ml	1 tbsp	1 tbsp
Eggs	2	2	2
Milk or single (light) cream	30 ml	2 tbsp	2 tbsp
Salt and pepper			
Grated Parmesan cheese and salad, to serve			

1 Fry (sauté) the onion, garlic and bacon in the oil for 2 minutes, cover and cook gently until the onion is soft.

2 Meanwhile, cook the spaghetti according to the packet directions, drain and return to the pan.

3 Stir in the bacon mixture and parsley. Beat the eggs with the milk or cream. Add to the pan. Toss over a gentle heat until creamy but do not boil or the egg will scramble. Season and serve with grated Parmesan cheese and salad.

PREPARATION TIME:
5–10 MINUTES

COOKING TIME:
ABOUT 15 MINUTES

POULTRY

Chicken and turkey are always excellent value for money and lend themselves to an infinite number of recipes.

Duck is a more expensive proposition but it has an exquisite flavour, well worth treating yourself to.

Chicken in Filo Pastry

SERVES 4	METRIC	IMPERIAL	AMERICAN
Boneless chicken breasts	4	4	4
Butter	25 g	1 oz	2 tbsp
Filo pastry (paste) sheets	4	4	4
Salt and pepper			
Cranberry sauce	40 ml	8 tsp	8 tsp
Can of asparagus spears	300 g	11 oz	1 small
Single (light) cream	30 ml	2 tbsp	2 tbsp
Grated nutmeg	1.5 ml	¼ tsp	¼ tsp
Parsley sprigs, to garnish			
A selection of young vegetables, to serve			

1 Fry (sauté) the chicken breasts in half the butter for 5 minutes until almost cooked, turning once.

2 Melt the remaining butter. Brush a little on the pastry sheets and fold in half.

3 Put 10 ml/2 tsp cranberry sauce in the centre of each sheet. Top with a chicken breast. Fold the pastry over.

4 Transfer to a buttered baking sheet, folded sides down, and brush with the remaining butter.

5 Bake in the oven at 200°C/400°F/gas mark 6 for about 15 minutes until golden brown.

6 Meanwhile, drain the asparagus, reserving the liquid, and sieve (strain) or liquidise. Place in a small pan and add the cream. Thin with a little of the reserved liquid, if necessary. Add the nutmeg and heat through.

7 Transfer the parcels to warm serving plates. Spoon a little of the sauce to one side and garnish with parsley. Serve with a selection of vegetables.

PREPARATION TIME:
10–15 MINUTES

COOKING TIME:
20 MINUTES

Cheesy Chicken Topper

SERVES 4	METRIC	IMPERIAL	AMERICAN
Chicken breast fillets	4	4	4
Butter, melted	20 g	¾ oz	1½ tbsp
Slices of lean ham	4	4	4
Gruyère (Swiss) or Cheddar cheese, grated	100 g	4 oz	1 cup
Tomato wedges and watercress, to garnish			
New potatoes and peas, to serve			

1 Place the chicken breasts in a plastic bag one at a time and beat with a rolling pin to flatten.

2 Brush the chicken breasts with melted butter and grill (broil) for 3 minutes on each side.

3 Trim the ham to fit the chicken. Place on top and cover liberally with the grated cheese.

4 Grill until the cheese is melted and turning golden.

5 Garnish with tomato wedges and watercress and serve with new potatoes and peas.

PREPARATION TIME:
10 MINUTES

COOKING TIME:
8–10 MINUTES

Chicken and Coconut Masala

SERVES 4	METRIC	IMPERIAL	AMERICAN
Boneless chicken meat, diced	350 g	12 oz	12 oz
Onion, chopped	1	1	1
Small green (bell) pepper, sliced	1	1	1
Mild curry powder	15 ml	1 tbsp	1 tbsp
Oil	30 ml	2 tbsp	2 tbsp
Chicken stock	450 ml	¾ pt	2 cups
Packet of creamed coconut	½	½	½
Ground almonds	30 ml	2 tbsp	2 tbsp
Raisins	15 ml	1 tbsp	1 tbsp
Salt and pepper			
Chopped coriander (cilantro)	15 ml	1 tbsp	1 tbsp
Lemon wedges, to garnish			
Pilau rice, to serve			

1 Fry (sauté) the chicken, onion, pepper and curry powder in the oil for 4 minutes, stirring.

2 Add the stock, coconut, ground almonds and raisins. Bring to the boil, reduce the heat and simmer for about 10 minutes until the chicken is cooked.

3 If sauce is still a little runny, remove the chicken with a draining spoon and boil the sauce rapidly, stirring, until reduced and thickened.

4 Season to taste. Return the chicken to the sauce and stir in the coriander.

5 Serve on a bed of pilau rice, garnished with lemon wedges.

PREPARATION TIME:
10 MINUTES

COOKING TIME:
14–20 MINUTES

Chicken Hawaii

You can substitute a can of pineapple chunks in natural juice, if you prefer, then serve the salad on a bed of lettuce.

SERVES 4	METRIC	IMPERIAL	AMERICAN
Fresh pineapple	1	1	1
Long-grain rice, cooked	175 g	6 oz	1½ cups
Cooked chicken, diced	175 g	6 oz	1½ cups
Can of sweetcorn (corn) with (bell) peppers, drained	198 g	7 oz	1 small
Mayonnaise	30 ml	2 tbsp	2 tbsp
Salt and pepper			
Lettuce leaves and tomato wedges, to garnish			
Green salad, to serve			

1 Cut the green top off the pineapple about 5 cm/2 in down from the stalk. Loosen the flesh with a serrated knife and scoop out into a bowl, leaving the shell intact.

2 Roughly chop the fruit, discarding any tough core. Drain off any excess juice. Place the fruit in a bowl.

3 Add the rice, chicken, sweetcorn and mayonnaise. Mix well and season to taste.

4 Pile the mixture back into the pineapple shell placed on a serving plate on a bed of lettuce. Put the green top back on as a 'lid'. Spoon any mixture that won't fit in the shell around the edge. Garnish with tomato wedges and serve with a green salad.

PREPARATION TIME:
15–20 MINUTES

Chinese-style Chicken with Cashew Nuts

SERVES 4	METRIC	IMPERIAL	AMERICAN
Boneless chicken thighs	225 g	8 oz	8 oz
Bunch of spring onions (scallions)	1	1	1
Oil	30 ml	2 tbsp	2 tbsp
Carrot, grated	1	1	1
Bean sprouts	275 g	10 oz	10 oz
Cashew nuts	25 g	1 oz	¼ cup
Chicken stock	300 ml	½ pt	1¼ cups
Cornflour (cornstarch)	15 ml	1 tbsp	1 tbsp
Soy sauce	15 ml	1 tbsp	1 tbsp
Fried rice, to serve			

1 Cut the meat into neat strips.

2 Trim the spring onions and chop into 2.5 cm/1 in pieces.

3 Heat the oil in a wok or large frying pan (skillet). Fry (sauté) the chicken, onions and carrot, stirring, for 5 minutes.

4 Add the bean sprouts and cook, stirring, for 3 minutes.

5 Add the cashew nuts and stock.

6 Blend the cornflour with the soy sauce and stir into the pan. Bring to the boil and cook for 2 minutes. Serve with fried rice.

PREPARATION TIME: 10–15 MINUTES

COOKING TIME: 10 MINUTES

Crunchy Turkey Escalopes

Replace the turkey breasts with chicken breasts or pieces of pork fillet for an equally tasty dish. Vary the flavour by using different stuffing mixes.

SERVES 4	METRIC	IMPERIAL	AMERICAN
Boneless turkey steaks	4	4	4
Egg, beaten	1	1	1
Packet of parsley and thyme stuffing mix	90 g	3½ oz	1 small
Oil for shallow-frying			
Lemon wedges and watercress, to garnish			
Puréed potatoes and French (green) beans, to serve			

1 Put a turkey breast in a plastic bag. Beat with a rolling pin to flatten. Repeat with the remaining pieces.

2 Dip the turkey breasts in beaten egg, then stuffing mix to coat completely.

3 Shallow-fry (sauté) in hot oil for about 3 minutes on each side until golden brown and cooked through.

4 Drain on kitchen paper. Transfer to warm serving plates. Garnish with lemon wedges and watercress and serve with puréed potatoes and French beans.

PREPARATION TIME: 10 MINUTES

COOKING TIME: 6 MINUTES

Duck Breasts with Orange

Two large duck breasts will be sufficient for four people – so this dish is not as extravagant as it may appear.

SERVES 4	METRIC	IMPERIAL	AMERICAN
Large duck breasts, skinned	2	2	2
Salt and pepper			
Butter	25 g	1 oz	2 tbsp
Brandy	15 ml	1 tbsp	1 tbsp
Chicken stock	150 ml	¼ pt	⅔ cup
Light brown sugar	5 ml	1 tsp	1 tsp
Grated rind and juice of 1 orange			
Cornflour (cornstarch)	15 ml	1 tbsp	1 tbsp
Watercress and orange twists, to garnish			
New potatoes and mangetout (snow peas), to serve			

1 Season the fillets, then fry (sauté) in the butter, turning occasionally, for 15 minutes until just pink in the centre (or a little longer, if you prefer it well cooked). Transfer to a warm dish and keep warm.

2 Add the brandy to the pan and ignite. When the flames subside, add the stock and sugar. Blend the orange rind and juice with the cornflour. Stir into the pan and bring to the boil, and cook, stirring, until thickened and clear. Season to taste.

3 Cut the duck into neat slices. Arrange attractively on four warm serving plates. Spoon the sauce over and garnish with watercress and orange twists. Serve with new potatoes and mangetout.

PREPARATION TIME:
5 MINUTES

COOKING TIME:
ABOUT 18 MINUTES

Fragrant Chicken Livers

SERVES 4	METRIC	IMPERIAL	AMERICAN
Onions, chopped	2	2	2
Butter	25 g	1 oz	2 tbsp
Oil	10 ml	2 tsp	2 tsp
Wineglass of medium sherry	1	1	1
Chicken livers, trimmed	450 g	1 lb	1 lb
Chopped sage	5 ml	1 tsp	1 tsp
Salt and pepper			
Buttered rice and leaf spinach, to serve			

1 Fry (sauté) the onions in the butter and oil for about 3 minutes until soft and golden.

2 Add the sherry and simmer, stirring, until the liquid has almost evaporated.

3 Add the livers, sage and a little salt and pepper. Cook, stirring, over a moderate heat for about 5 minutes until the livers are cooked but still tender.

4 Serve with buttered rice and leaf spinach.

PREPARATION TIME:
5–10 MINUTES

COOKING TIME:
8 MINUTES

Spaghetti with Turkey and Mushrooms

SERVES 4	METRIC	IMPERIAL	AMERICAN
Olive oil	60 ml	4 tbsp	4 tbsp
Boneless turkey, diced	175 g	6 oz	6 oz
Carrot, finely chopped	1	1	1
Celery stick, finely chopped	1	1	1
Onion, finely chopped	1	1	1
Garlic clove, crushed	1	1	1
Button mushrooms, sliced	100 g	4 oz	4 oz
Tomatoes, chopped	4	4	4
Frozen peas	50 g	2 oz	2 oz
Spaghetti	350 g	12 oz	12 oz
Salt and pepper			
Grated Parmesan cheese, to serve			

1 Heat the oil in a large pan. Fry (sauté) all the ingredients except the spaghetti for 3 minutes, stirring. Reduce the heat, cover and cook gently for about 10 minutes, stirring occasionally until cooked through.

2 Meanwhile, cook the spaghetti according to the packet directions. Drain. Add to the turkey mixture and toss well.

3 Serve hot with grated Parmesan cheese.

PREPARATION TIME:
10 MINUTES

COOKING TIME:
13–15 MINUTES

Spanish Rice

You can use up cooked chicken or turkey in this dish but the flavour won't be quite as good. Any leftovers are delicious cold.

SERVES 4	METRIC	IMPERIAL	AMERICAN
Boneless chicken, diced	175 g	6 oz	6 oz
Small green (bell) pepper, diced	1	1	1
Small red pepper, diced	1	1	1
Olive oil	30 ml	2 tbsp	2 tbsp
Long-grain rice	225 g	8 oz	1 cup
Chicken stock	600 ml	1 pt	2½ cups
Frozen peas with sweetcorn (corn)	100 g	4 oz	4 oz
Peeled prawns (shrimp)	100 g	4 oz	4 oz
Salt and pepper			

A few black olives and chopped parsley, to garnish

1 Fry (sauté) the chicken and peppers in the oil for 4 minutes, stirring.

2 Add the rice and stir for 1 minute.

3 Pour on the stock, bring to the boil, cover and simmer for 10 minutes.

4 Add the peas and sweetcorn and prawns, re-cover and cook for a further 10 minutes until the rice is cooked and has absorbed nearly all the liquid. Season to taste.

5 Serve garnished with olives and chopped parsley.

PREPARATION TIME:
10 MINUTES

COOKING TIME:
25 MINUTES

MEATLESS MEALS

*You don't have to be a vegetarian to enjoy
meals without meat. The following recipes are
all very nutritious and exceptionally tasty
too. Don't forget, if you are serving them to
vegetarians, to make sure you use vegetarian
cheese or one that's suitable for them to eat
(it's usually marked on the packet).*

Caesar Salad Special

SERVES 4	METRIC	IMPERIAL	AMERICAN
Butter	15 g	½ oz	1 tbsp
Egg, beaten	1	1	1
Soft cheese with garlic and herbs	75 g	3 oz	⅓ cup
Milk	45 ml	3 tbsp	3 tbsp
Olive oil	15 ml	1 tbsp	1 tbsp
Lemon juice	10 ml	2 tsp	2 tsp
Cos (romaine) lettuce	1	1	1
Can of anchovies, drained and chopped	50 g	2 oz	1 small
Slices of French bread, fried (sautéed) in a little olive oil	8	8	8
Tomato wedges, to garnish			

1 Melt the butter in a pan. Add the egg and scramble lightly over a gentle heat. Remove from the heat and leave to cool.

2 Whisk the cheese with the milk, oil and lemon juice until smooth.

3 Tear the lettuce into neat pieces and place in a salad bowl.

4 Add the egg and anchovies, pour the dressing over and toss.

5 Arrange the slices of fried French bread around the edge of the bowl and garnish with tomato wedges.

PREPARATION TIME: 15 MINUTES

COOKING TIME: 3 MINUTES

No-nonsense Ratatouille

SERVES 4	METRIC	IMPERIAL	AMERICAN
Small aubergine (eggplant), sliced	1	1	1
Courgettes (zucchini), sliced	3	3	3
Onion, sliced	1	1	1
Green (bell) pepper, sliced	1	1	1
Tomatoes, chopped	4	4	4
Olive oil	45 ml	3 tbsp	3 tbsp
Dried oregano	2.5 ml	½ tsp	½ tsp
Salt and pepper			
Tomato purée (paste)	15 ml	1 tbsp	1 tbsp
Red wine or water	30 ml	2 tbsp	2 tbsp
Buttered pasta and grated Parmesan cheese, to serve			

1 Put the prepared vegetables in a large pan with the olive oil. Cook, stirring, for 5 minutes until they begin to soften.

2 Add the oregano, seasoning and the tomato purée blended with the wine or water. Cover and simmer for 15 minutes, stirring occasionally, until the vegetables are just tender.

3 Serve with buttered pasta and grated Parmesan cheese.

PREPARATION TIME:
10 MINUTES

COOKING TIME:
20 MINUTES

Cucumber and Potato Gratin

SERVES 4	METRIC	IMPERIAL	AMERICAN
Potatoes, diced	450 g	1 lb	1 lb
Cucumbers, in bite-sized chunks	2	2	2
White wine	150 ml	¼ pt	⅔ cup
Milk	300 ml	½ pt	1¼ cups
Butter or margarine	25 g	1 oz	2 tbsp
Plain (all-purpose) flour	25 g	1 oz	¼ cup
Cheddar cheese, grated	175 g	6 oz	1½ cups
Salt and pepper			
Dijon mustard	5 ml	1 tsp	1 tsp
Beetroot (red beet), walnut and celery salad, to serve			

1 Cook the potatoes in boiling water for about
   4–5 minutes until just tender. Drain.

2 Put the cucumber in a pan with the wine. Cover and
   cook for about 8–10 minutes until tender. Remove
   the cucumber from the wine with a draining spoon.

3 Add the milk to the wine, then whisk in the butter
   and flour. Bring to the boil and cook for 2 minutes,
   whisking all the time.

4 Stir in half the cheese and season to taste with salt,
   pepper and mustard. Fold in the cooked potatoes and
   cucumber and heat through.

5 Turn into a lightly buttered flameproof dish and
   sprinkle with the remaining cheese. Grill (broil) until
   golden and bubbling. Serve hot with a beetroot,
   walnut and celery salad.

PREPARATION TIME:
10 MINUTES

COOKING TIME:
15–20 MINUTES

Pizza Parcels

SERVES 4	METRIC	IMPERIAL	AMERICAN
Filo pastry (paste) sheets	4	4	4
Butter, melted	15 g	½ oz	1 tbsp
Canned pimiento, chopped	1	1	1
Mushrooms, sliced	4	4	4
Tomatoes, sliced	2	2	2
Basil leaves	8	8	8
Pepper			
Mozzarella cheese, grated	100 g	4 oz	1 cup
A few basil leaves and black olives, to garnish			
Ciabatta bread and green salad, to serve			

1 Brush each pastry sheet with a very little butter. Fold in half and brush again.

2 Divide the pimiento, mushrooms and tomato slices between the pastry sheets. Top with torn basil leaves, some pepper and the grated cheese.

3 Draw the pastry up over the filling to form parcels, squeezing between finger and thumb to secure. Transfer to a buttered baking sheet and brush with the remaining butter.

4 Bake in the oven at 200°C/400°F/gas mark 6 for about 12–15 minutes until golden.

5 Transfer to warm plates. Garnish with basil leaves and olives and serve straight away with ciabatta bread and a green salad.

PREPARATION TIME: 10 MINUTES

COOKING TIME: 12–15 MINUTES

Regatta Rice Ring

SERVES 4	METRIC	IMPERIAL	AMERICAN
Long-grain rice	175 g	6 oz	¾ cup
Frozen mixed diced vegetables	100 g	4 oz	4 oz
Olive oil	30 ml	2 tbsp	2 tbsp
Wine vinegar	15 ml	1 tbsp	1 tbsp
Salt and pepper			
Ripe pears, diced	2	2	2
Cheddar cheese, diced	175 g	6 oz	6 oz
Head of Florence fennel, chopped	1	1	1
Plain yoghurt	45 ml	3 tbsp	3 tbsp
Garlic bread, to serve			

1 Cook the rice and mixed vegetables in plenty of lightly salted boiling water for 10 minutes. Drain, rinse thoroughly with cold water and drain again.

2 Add the oil, vinegar and a little salt and pepper to the rice and vegetables and toss well.

3 Spoon the mixture into a 1.5 litre/2½ pt/6 cup oiled ring mould. Press down well and chill in the freezer while making the filling.

4 Mix the pears with the cheese and fennel (saving the green feathery leaves for decoration). Gently fold in the yoghurt and season lightly.

5 Place a serving plate over the ring mould. Invert, give a good shake and remove the mould. Pile the cheese and pear mixture in the centre and garnish with the fennel leaves before serving with garlic bread.

PREPARATION TIME: 15 MINUTES

COOKING TIME: 10 MINUTES

Pissaladière

Use a processor to make the pastry (paste) in an instant.

SERVES 4	METRIC	IMPERIAL	AMERICAN
Plain (all-purpose) flour	175 g	6 oz	1½ cups
Ground cinnamon	5 ml	1 tsp	1 tsp
Butter	75 g	3 oz	⅓ cup
Onions, chopped	3	3	3
Garlic clove, crushed	1	1	1
Olive oil	30 ml	2 tbsp	2 tbsp
Tomatoes, roughly chopped	450 g	1 lb	1 lb
Tomato purée (paste)	15 ml	1 tbsp	1 tbsp
Caster (superfine) sugar	2.5 ml	½ tsp	½ tsp
Salt and pepper			
Can of anchovy fillets, drained	50 g	2 oz	1 small
Black olives	6	6	6
Chopped parsley, to garnish			
Green salad, to serve			

1 Mix together the flour and cinnamon. Rub in the butter and mix with enough cold water to form a firm dough.

2 Roll out and use to line a 20 cm/8 in flan dish (pie pan).

3 Prick the base with a fork, add some crumpled foil and bake 'blind' for 8 minutes in the oven at 200°C/400°F/gas mark 6. Remove the foil and cook for a further 4 minutes.

4 Meanwhile, soften the onion and garlic in the oil for 2 minutes in a large pan. Add the tomatoes, stir, cover and cook for 8 minutes until pulpy. Stir in the tomato purée, sugar and a little salt and pepper.

5 Turn into the pastry case (pie shell). Spread out and decorate in a criss-cross pattern with the anchovies and the olives. Return to the oven for 10 minutes. Garnish with chopped parsley and serve with a green salad.

PREPARATION TIME:
10–15 MINUTES

COOKING TIME:
22 MINUTES

Spaghetti with Green Herbs and Mushrooms

SERVES 4	METRIC	IMPERIAL	AMERICAN
Butter	50 g	2 oz	¼ cup
Mushrooms, sliced	100 g	4 oz	4 oz
Garlic clove, crushed	1	1	1
Ground almonds	50 g	2 oz	½ cup
Grated Parmesan cheese	30 ml	2 tbsp	2 tbsp
Olive oil	30 ml	2 tbsp	2 tbsp
Chopped parsley	30 ml	2 tbsp	2 tbsp
Chopped sage	10 ml	2 tsp	2 tsp
Chopped oregano	15 ml	1 tbsp	1 tbsp
Salt and pepper			
Spaghetti	350 g	12 oz	12 oz
Tomato and onion salad, to serve			

1 Melt half the butter in a pan and fry (sauté) the mushrooms gently for 3 minutes. Put to one side.

2 Mash the remaining butter with the garlic, almonds and cheese. Gradually work in the oil, herbs and seasoning.

3 Cook the spaghetti according to the packet directions. Drain, return to the saucepan and add the mushrooms and the herb mixture.

4 Toss over a gentle heat until the spaghetti is well coated in the sauce. Serve hot with salad.

PREPARATION TIME: 10 MINUTES

COOKING TIME: 12–15 MINUTES

Sicilian Salad

This is delicious with the addition of prawns (shrimp) or tuna fish.

SERVES 4	METRIC	IMPERIAL	AMERICAN
Dwarf green beans, cooked whole	225 g	8 oz	8 oz
Baby new potatoes, cooked	225 g	8 oz	8 oz
Tomatoes, quartered	4	4	4
Eggs, hard-boiled (hard-cooked), and quartered	3	3	3
Small onion, sliced and separated into rings	1	1	1
Black or green olives	6	6	6
Olive oil	45 ml	3 tbsp	3 tbsp
Wine vinegar	15 ml	1 tbsp	1 tbsp
Salt and pepper			
Crisp lettuce	1	1	1
Goats' cheese, diced	75 g	3 oz	3 oz
Crusty bread, to serve			

1 Cut the beans and potatoes into two or three pieces. Place in a bowl with the remaining ingredients except the lettuce and cheese and toss lightly.

2 Pile on to a bed of crisp lettuce and scatter the cheese over. Serve with crusty bread.

PREPARATION TIME:
10 MINUTES

Watercress Roulade

This recipe also makes a delicious starter for six to eight people.

SERVES 4	METRIC	IMPERIAL	AMERICAN
Onion, chopped	1	1	1
Olive oil	15 ml	1 tbsp	1 tbsp
Tomatoes, chopped	4	4	4
Tomato purée (paste)	15 ml	1 tbsp	1 tbsp
Caster (superfine) sugar	5 ml	1 tsp	1 tsp
Bunch of watercress, chopped	1	1	1
Snipped chives	15 ml	1 tbsp	1 tbsp
Grated Parmesan cheese	45 ml	3 tbsp	3 tbsp
Eggs, separated	4	4	4
Raisin, nut and rice salad, to serve			

1 Fry (sauté) the onion in the oil for 2 minutes to soften. Add the tomatoes, cover and cook gently for 5 minutes or until pulpy. Add the purée and sugar and season to taste. Keep warm.

2 Meanwhile, grease an 18×28 cm/7×11 in Swiss roll tin (jelly roll pan). Line with baking parchment.

3 Wash the watercress and chop finely. Mix together with the chives, 30 ml/2 tbsp of the Parmesan and a little seasoning. Beat in the egg yolks.

4 Whisk the egg whites until stiff and fold into the watercress mixture with a metal spoon.

5 Turn the mixture into the prepared tin, smooth the surface and cook towards the top of the oven at 200°C/400°F/gas mark 6 for about 10 minutes until golden and firm to touch.

6 Dust a sheet of baking parchment with the remaining Parmesan. Turn the roulade out on to this and remove the lining paper, easing it away with a palette knife. Spread with the tomato mixture and roll up from one short end, using the parchment to help.

7 Transfer the roulade to a warm serving dish and serve sliced with a raisin, nut and rice salad.

PREPARATION TIME:
20 MINUTES

COOKING TIME:
10 MINUTES

SNACKS & LIGHT MEALS

When you fancy a quick bite, you do not have

to turn to pot noodles or cup-a-soups.

Here is a range of tempting light lunch

and supper dishes to show you that

fast food can be fantastic.

Cheese Dream

SERVES 1	METRIC	IMPERIAL	AMERICAN
Slices of bread	2	2	2
Butter for spreading			
Cheddar cheese, grated	40 g	1½ oz	⅓ cup
Small onion, sliced and separated into rings	½	½	½
Chopped sage	5 ml	1 tsp	1 tsp

1 Liberally butter the slices of bread on one side.

2 Sandwich together, buttered sides out, with the cheese, onion and sage.

3 Fry (sauté) or grill (broil) until golden on both sides. Serve straight away, cut into quarters.

PREPARATION TIME:
3–5 MINUTES

COOKING TIME:
5 MINUTES

Devilled Mushrooms

SERVES 2	METRIC	IMPERIAL	AMERICAN
Small onion, finely chopped	1	1	1
Oil	15 ml	1 tbsp	1 tbsp
Button mushrooms	175 g	6 oz	6 oz
Tomatoes, skinned, if preferred, and chopped	2	2	2
Tomato ketchup (catsup)	10 ml	2 tsp	2 tsp
Worcestershire sauce	10 ml	2 tsp	2 tsp
Drops of Tabasco sauce	1–2	1–2	1–2
Hot buttered toast, to serve			

1 Fry (sauté) the onion in the oil for 2 minutes until softened. Add the mushrooms and tomatoes and cook, stirring for 2 minutes.

2 Add the remaining ingredients and simmer for about 5 minutes or until the mushrooms are just cooked.

3 Serve on hot buttered toast.

PREPARATION TIME:
5 MINUTES

COOKING TIME:
9 MINUTES

Macaroni Masterpiece

SERVES 2	METRIC	IMPERIAL	AMERICAN
Streaky bacon rashers (slices)	4	4	4
Quick-cook macaroni	100 g	4 oz	4 oz
Red Leicester cheese, grated	100 g	4 oz	1 cup
Worcestershire sauce	5 ml	1 tsp	1 tsp
Salt and pepper			
Butter, melted	25 g	1 oz	2 tbsp
Snipped chives, to garnish			

1 Grill (broil) or dry-fry (sauté) the bacon until crisp. Cut into pieces.

2 Meanwhile, cook the macaroni according to the packet directions, drain and return to the pan.

3 Add the cheese, Worcestershire sauce, a little seasoning and the butter. Toss well until creamy.

4 Pile on to warm serving plates and serve sprinkled with the bacon and chives.

PREPARATION TIME:
5 MINUTES

COOKING TIME:
ABOUT 10 MINUTES

Melting Crescents

As an alternative, you can spread the croissant with soft garlic and herb cheese and add some chopped red (bell) pepper before grilling (broiling).

SERVES 1	METRIC	IMPERIAL	AMERICAN
Croissant	1	1	1
Slices of salami	2	2	2
Slice of Emmental or Gruyère (Swiss) cheese	1	1	1
Slices of tomato, to serve			

1 Split the croissant almost in half and fill with the folded salami and cheese.

2 Place under a moderate grill (broiler) until the cheese melts, turning once. Serve with tomato slices.

PREPARATION TIME: 2 MINUTES COOKING TIME: ABOUT 3 MINUTES

Pan Pizza

You can add toppings of your choice to this pizza, such as diced ham, sliced mushrooms or tuna.

SERVES 1 OR 2	METRIC	IMPERIAL	AMERICAN
Self-raising (self-rising) flour	100 g	4 oz	1 cup
Salt			
Sunflower oil	45 ml	3 tbsp	3 tbsp
Can of chopped tomatoes, drained	227 g	8 oz	1 small
Cheddar cheese, grated	50 g	2 oz	½ cup
Dried oregano	1.5 ml	¼ tsp	¼ tsp
A few black olives, to garnish			

1 Mix the flour, salt and 30 ml/2 tbsp of the oil in a bowl. Add enough cold water to form a firm dough and knead gently.

2 Roll or press out to a round to roughly fit the base of a medium frying pan (skillet).

3 Heat the remaining oil in the frying pan, add the dough and fry for 1 minute. Turn over and spread with the tomatoes.

4 Top with the cheese and sprinkle with oregano. Garnish with olives. Cover with a lid or foil and cook over a gentle heat for 5 minutes until the cheese is melting. Place under a hot grill (broiler) to brown the top.

PREPARATION TIME: 8–10 MINUTES

COOKING TIME: ABOUT 8 MINUTES

Pitta Pocket Cooler

SERVES 1	METRIC	IMPERIAL	AMERICAN
Piece of cucumber, chopped	2.5 cm	1 in	1 in
Chopped cooked lamb	15 ml	1 tbsp	1 tbsp
Plain yoghurt	15 ml	1 tbsp	1 tbsp
Mint, dried	1.5 ml	¼ tsp	¼ tsp
Salt and pepper			
Pitta bread	1	1	1
A few lettuce leaves			
Tomato, sliced	1	1	1

1 Mix together the cucumber, lamb, yoghurt and mint. Season to taste.

2 Warm the pitta bread briefly under the grill (broiler) or in a toaster, if liked.

3 Make a slit along one long edge to form a pocket. Fill with lettuce leaves, then add the yoghurt mixture and some tomato slices.

PREPARATION TIME: 5–8 MINUTES.

Saucy Ham 'n' Eggs

SERVES 2	METRIC	IMPERIAL	AMERICAN
Bunch of watercress, chopped	1	1	1
Butter or margarine	15 g	½ oz	1 tbsp
Plain (all-purpose) flour	15 g	½ oz	2 tbsp
Milk	150 ml	¼ pt	⅔ cup
Salt and pepper			
Eggs	2	2	2
Lemon juice or vinegar	5 ml	1 tsp	1 tsp
Slices of ham	2	2	2
Slices of buttered toast	2	2	2

1 Put the watercress, fat, flour and milk in a saucepan. Whisk over a moderate heat until thickened and smooth. Season to taste.

2 Poach the eggs in water with the lemon juice or vinegar added for 3–5 minutes to the consistency you like.

3 Put a slice of ham on each of the slices of toast.

4 Top with a poached egg. Spoon the hot watercress sauce over and serve straight away.

PREPARATION TIME: 5–10 MINUTES COOKING TIME: 5 MINUTES

Somerset Rarebit

You can substitute beer or white wine for the cider. Double the quantity for a quick cheese fondue to serve with cubes of French bread.

SERVES 1 OR 2	METRIC	IMPERIAL	AMERICAN
Cheddar cheese, grated	175 g	6 oz	1½ cups
Made English mustard	5 ml	1 tsp	1 tsp
Cider	30 ml	2 tbsp	2 tbsp
Slices of toast	2	2	2

1 Put all the ingredients except the toast in a small pan. Heat gently, stirring, until the cheese has melted and mixture is well blended.

2 Spoon on to the toast and serve.

PREPARATION TIME: 5 MINUTES

COOKING TIME: ABOUT 5 MINUTES

Spicy Potato Cakes

*These potato cakes also make a delicious starter for four
people, served before Tandoori Fish (page 56),
Eastern Lamb (page 70) or Chicken and Coconut Masala
(page 94).*

SERVES 2	METRIC	IMPERIAL	AMERICAN
Potatoes, grated	225 g	8 oz	8 oz
Small onion, grated	1	1	1
Garam masala	2.5 ml	½ tsp	½ tsp
Chilli powder	1.5 ml	¼ tsp	¼ tsp
Egg, beaten	1	1	1
Plain (all-purpose) flour	15 ml	1 tbsp	1 tbsp
Salt and pepper			
Oil	30 ml	2 tbsp	2 tbsp
Mango chutney, to serve			

1 Mix together the potato, onion, spices, egg and flour,
   seasoning to taste.

2 Heat the oil in a frying pan (skillet) and fry (sauté)
   tablespoonfuls of the mixture until golden brown
   underneath. Turn over and fry the other side.

3 Serve hot with mango chutney.

PREPARATION TIME:
5–8 MINUTES

COOKING TIME:
5 MINUTES

Tortilla

This can be made with leftover cooked potato. Tortilla is delicious served cold with salad.

SERVES 2	METRIC	IMPERIAL	AMERICAN
Large potato, thinly sliced	*1*	*1*	*1*
Small onion, chopped	*1*	*1*	*1*
Olive oil	*15 ml*	*1 tbsp*	*1 tbsp*
Chopped parsley	*15 ml*	*1 tbsp*	*1 tbsp*
Salt and pepper			
Eggs, beaten	*4*	*4*	*4*

1 Put the potato and onion in a frying pan (skillet) and fry (sauté), stirring, in the oil for 4 minutes, until the potato is almost cooked.

2 Add the parsley, a little seasoning and the eggs. Cook gently, lifting and stirring at first until the egg has almost set. Place under a hot grill (broiler) to brown and set the top. Serve cut into wedges.

PREPARATION TIME: 5 MINUTES

COOKING TIME: ABOUT 10 MINUTES

DESSERTS

For many people the crowning glory of a meal
is the dessert. It may be hot or cold, rich or
fruity but most of all it should be easy to
make and look and taste superb.

Fruit makes wonderful, easy desserts. A bowl
of diced melon and raspberries sprinkled
with sugar and finely chopped mint looks
and tastes wonderful. Or you can serve
melon balls chilled in a few tablespoons of
ginger wine and topped with ice cream. If
you enjoy the wine connection, serve sliced
nectarines in wine goblets topped up with
sparkling wine. For the chocoholics, dip half
of wedges of firm fruit in melted chocolate,
then chill.

Bananas with Hot Lemon Butter Sauce

Use ice cream instead of yoghurt, if you prefer.

SERVES 4	METRIC	IMPERIAL	AMERICAN
Butter	50 g	2 oz	¼ cup
Light brown sugar	75 g	3 oz	⅓ cup
Lemon juice	30 ml	2 tbsp	2 tbsp
Greek-style plain yoghurt	300 ml	½ pt	1¼ cups
Bananas, sliced	4	4	4
Toasted flaked (slivered) almonds, to decorate			

1 Put the butter, sugar and lemon juice in a small pan. Heat gently, stirring, until the sugar has melted. Simmer for 1 minute.

2 Divide the yoghurt between four sundae glasses. Top with banana slices.

3 Spoon the sauce over and decorate with toasted almonds. Serve straight away.

PREPARATION TIME: 5 MINUTES

COOKING TIME: ABOUT 3 MINUTES

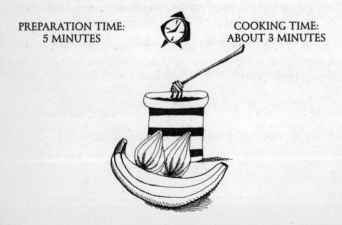

Caribbean Bananas

SERVES 4	METRIC	IMPERIAL	AMERICAN
Orange	*1*	*1*	*1*
Cocoa (unsweetened chocolate) *powder*	*45 ml*	*3 tbsp*	*3 tbsp*
Light brown sugar	*45 ml*	*3 tbsp*	*3 tbsp*
Pinch of ground cinnamon			
Rum or orange liqueur	*45 ml*	*3 tbsp*	*3 tbsp*
Bananas	*4*	*4*	*4*
Whipped cream or fromage frais, to serve			

1 Cut four slices from the orange and reserve for decoration. Grate the rind and squeeze the juice from the remainder into a frying pan (skillet).

2 Add the cocoa powder and sugar and heat gently, stirring, until the sugar melts. Add the rum or orange liqueur.

3 Peel the bananas and cut into chunks. Add to the pan. Spoon the sauce over, cover with foil or a lid and cook gently for 4 minutes or until the bananas are just cooked but still hold their shape.

4 Spoon into serving dishes, decorate each with a slice of orange and serve hot or cold with whipped cream or fromage frais.

PREPARATION TIME:
5 MINUTES

COOKING TIME:
ABOUT 8 MINUTES

Blackberry and Apple Layer

When blackberries are not in season, use canned or frozen fruit instead.

SERVES 4–6	METRIC	IMPERIAL	AMERICAN
Cooking (tart) apples, sliced	450 g	1 lb	1 lb
Blackberries	100 g	4 oz	4 oz
Caster (superfine) sugar, to taste			
Trifle sponge cakes	4	4	4
Cider or apple juice	30 ml	2 tbsp	2 tbsp
Whipping cream	150 ml	¼ pt	⅔ cup
Vanilla-flavoured thick yoghurt	300 ml	½ pt	1¼ cups

1 Put the apples in a pan. Choose a few blackberries for decoration, if liked, then add the remainder to the pan with 15 ml/1 tbsp water. Cover and cook gently for about 5 minutes until just soft and the juice has run. Sweeten to taste.

2 Crumble the trifle sponges into a glass serving bowl. Add the fruit and drizzle cider or apple juice over. Leave to cool.

3 Whip the cream and fold in the yoghurt. Spread over the fruit and decorate with the reserved blackberries.

PREPARATION TIME:
10 MINUTES
PLUS COOLING TIME

COOKING TIME:
5 MINUTES

Caramel Apples

SERVES 4	METRIC	IMPERIAL	AMERICAN
Butter	50 g	2 oz	¼ cup
Eating (dessert) apples, sliced	4	4	4
Light brown sugar	50 g	2 oz	¼ cup
Mixed (apple-pie) spice	2.5 ml	½ tsp	½ tsp
Sultanas (golden raisins)	30 ml	2 tbsp	2 tbsp
Walnuts or pecans, chopped	25 g	1 oz	¼ cup
Whipped cream or Greek-style yoghurt, to serve			

1 Melt the butter in a frying pan (skillet).

2 Add the apples and sprinkle with the sugar. Fry (sauté), tossing occasionally, for about 3 minutes until the sugar has melted.

3 Add the sultanas and nuts and toss gently. Serve with whipped cream or Greek-style yoghurt.

PREPARATION TIME:
5 MINUTES

COOKING TIME:
5 MINUTES

Chocolate Mousse

To make chocolate curls, scrape a potato peeler along the edge of a bar of chocolate several times.

SERVES 6	METRIC	IMPERIAL	AMERICAN
Plain (semi-sweet) chocolate	200 g	7 oz	7 oz
Eggs, separated	3	3	3
Brandy	15 ml	1 tbsp	1 tbsp
Whipping cream	150 ml	¼ pt	⅔ cup
Chocolate curls, to decorate			

1 Melt the chocolate in a bowl over a pan of hot water or in the microwave. Beat in the egg yolks and brandy.

2 In separate bowls, whisk the egg whites and then the cream until peaking (this means you do not have to wash the beaters in between). Fold the cream, then the egg whites, into the chocolate mixture.

3 Turn into a serving dish, sprinkle with chocolate curls and chill until ready to serve.

PREPARATION TIME:
10 MINUTES
PLUS CHILLING TIME

Frinklies

Pop these in the oven when you dish up the main course as they're best eaten freshly cooked.

SERVES 4	METRIC	IMPERIAL	AMERICAN
Soft margarine	50 g	2 oz	¼ cup
Caster (superfine) sugar	50 g	2 oz	¼ cup
Eggs	2	2	2
Plain (all-purpose) flour	50 g	2 oz	½ cup
Milk	150 ml	¼ pt	⅔ cup

Warm jam (conserve) or clear honey

Sifted icing (confectioners') sugar, for dusting

1 Beat the margarine, caster sugar, eggs and flour together, then stir in the milk. (Do not worry if the mixture curdles.)

2 Spoon into 12 sections of a greased bun tin (muffin pan).

3 Bake in the oven at 200°C/400°F/gas mark 6 for about 15–20 minutes until set and golden. They will sink when they're taken out of the oven – but don't worry, they're supposed to!

4 Arrange three frinklies slightly overlapping on each serving plate. Spoon a little warmed jam or clear honey over and dust with icing sugar before serving.

PREPARATION TIME:
5 MINUTES

COOKING TIME:
15–20 MINUTES

Fruit Brulée

You can also use sliced stoned (pitted) fruit like peaches, plums or nectarines.

SERVES 4	METRIC	IMPERIAL	AMERICAN
Strawberries, sliced, or raspberries	*225 g*	*8 oz*	*8 oz*
Double (heavy) cream	*150 ml*	*¼ pt*	*⅔ cup*
Thick plain yoghurt	*150 ml*	*¼ pt*	*⅔ cup*
Light brown sugar			

1 Arrange the fruit in a shallow flameproof dish.

2 Whip together the cream and yoghurt until softly peaking. Spread over the fruit. Chill, if time allows.

3 Sprinkle liberally with sugar so it covers the top completely.

4 Place under a very hot grill (broiler) until the sugar melts. Serve straight away.

PREPARATION TIME:
5 MINUTES
PLUS CHILLING TIME

COOKING TIME:
ABOUT 3 MINUTES

Jalousie

SERVES 6–8	METRIC	IMPERIAL	AMERICAN
Puff pastry (paste), thawed if frozen	225 g	8 oz	8 oz
Black cherry jam (conserve)	60 ml	4 tbsp	4 tbsp
Milk, to glaze			
Sifted icing (confectioners') sugar, to decorate			
Whipped cream, to serve			

1 Halve the pastry and roll one half out to a rectangle about 20×25 cm/8×10 in. Transfer to a dampened baking sheet.

2 Roll out the other half to the same size. Dust with a little flour, then fold in half lengthways. Make a series of cuts along the folded edge to within 2.5 cm/1 in of the open edge (like the paper lanterns you made as a child).

3 Spread the uncut rectangle generously with jam, leaving a 2.5 cm/1 in border all round. Brush the edges with water, then carefully unfold the cut rectangle and lay over the top, pressing the edges well together to seal.

4 Bake in the oven at 220°C/425°F/gas mark 7 for about 15 minutes until golden and puffy. Dust with icing sugar and serve warm with whipped cream.

PREPARATION TIME:
10–15 MINUTES

COOKING TIME:
15 MINUTES

Lemon Dream

Eaten straight away, this dessert is creamy and light. Chill for several hours and you'll have a syllabub-effect – fluffy on the top, juicy underneath.

SERVES 6	METRIC	IMPERIAL	AMERICAN
Egg white	1	1	1
Caster (superfine) sugar	75 g	3 oz	⅓ cup
Double (heavy) cream	150 g	¼ pt	⅔ cup
Grated rind and juice of 1 lemon			
Thick plain yoghurt	300 ml	½ pt	1¼ cups
Crystallised (candied) violets or lemon slices and angelica leaves, to decorate			

1 Whisk the egg white until stiff, then whisk in half the sugar.

2 Whip the cream, lemon rind and juice and the remaining sugar until softly peaking. Gently whisk or fold in the yoghurt. Finally fold in the egg white with a metal spoon.

3 Spoon into six wine goblets and chill, if liked. Just before serving, top each with a crystallised violet or lemon slice and an angelica leaf.

PREPARATION TIME:
10 MINUTES
PLUS CHILLING TIME

Mango Fool

This dessert is best eaten soon after it is made.

SERVES 4	METRIC	IMPERIAL	AMERICAN
Mango	1	1	1
Lemon juice	45 ml	3 tbsp	3 tbsp
Caster (superfine) sugar	15 ml	1 tbsp	1 tbsp
Can of custard	425 g	15 oz	1 large
Whipped cream	150 ml	¼ pt	⅔ cup
Angelica leaves, to decorate			

1 Peel the mango and cut all the flesh off the stone (pit). Purée in a blender or processor with the lemon juice and sugar.

2 Fold in the custard and half the cream.

3 Spoon into four wine goblets. Decorate each with a swirl of the remaining whipped cream and an angelica leaf. Eat within 2 hours.

PREPARATION TIME:
10 MINUTES

Orange Raffles

SERVES 6	METRIC	IMPERIAL	AMERICAN
Oranges	6	6	6
Trifle sponges	3	3	3
Sherry	30 ml	2 tbsp	2 tbsp
Double (heavy) or whipping cream	250 ml	8 fl oz	1 cup
Caster (superfine) sugar	30 ml	2 tbsp	2 tbsp
A few drops of vanilla essence (extract)			
Toasted flaked (slivered) almonds, to decorate			

1 Cut the rounded ends off the oranges (they will stand up better on the stalk end) and scoop out the flesh with a serrated knife.

2 Chop fairly finely and place in a bowl with any juice.

3 Crumble in the trifle sponges and add the sherry. Mix well and spoon back into the orange shells.

4 Whip the cream with the sugar and vanilla until softly peaking. Pipe or swirl on top of each orange. Sprinkle with nuts and chill, if there is time, until ready to serve.

PREPARATION TIME:
10 MINUTES
PLUS CHILLING TIME

Pear and Ginger Strudels

If you don't like ginger, try substituting chocolate chips.

SERVES 4	METRIC	IMPERIAL	AMERICAN
Ripe pears, chopped	2	2	2
Pieces of stem ginger in syrup, chopped	2	2	2
Filo pastry (paste) sheets	4	4	4
Melted butter	15 ml	1 tbsp	1 tbsp

1 Mix together the pears and ginger.

2 Brush the sheets of pastry with a little butter, fold in half and brush with a little more butter.

3 Divide the pear mixture between the pastry sheets, putting it in the middle of one edge. Fold each side of the pastry over the filling, then roll up. Brush with any remaining butter.

4 Transfer to a lightly buttered baking sheet and bake in the oven at 190°C/375°F/gas mark 5 for 10–15 minutes until golden. Serve warm with a little syrup from the jar of ginger spooned over.

PREPARATION TIME:
10–15 MINUTES

COOKING TIME:
10–15 MINUTES

Pink Grapefruit Cheesecake

This recipe is equally delicious with other citrus fruit. If you haven't time to chill the cheesecake in the fridge, pop it in the freezer compartment for 15 minutes instead.

SERVES 6	METRIC	IMPERIAL	AMERICAN
Chocolate digestive biscuits (graham crackers), crushed	200 g	7 oz	scant 2 cups
Butter, melted	50 g	2 oz	¼ cup
Curd (smooth cottage) cheese	500 g	1 lb 2 oz	2¼ cups
Icing (confectioners') sugar, sifted	40 g	1½ oz	¼ cup
Grated rind and juice of 1 pink grapefruit			
Lemon juice	15 ml	1 tbsp	1 tbsp
Ground almonds	50 g	2 oz	½ cup
Grated chocolate, to decorate			

1 Mix the biscuits with the butter and press into a lightly buttered 18–20 cm/7–8 in flan dish (pie pan).

2 Beat together the cheese, sugar, grapefruit rind and juice, lemon juice and almonds. Spoon over the biscuit base.

3 Top with a little grated chocolate and chill until ready to serve, allowing 30 minutes, preferably longer.

PREPARATION TIME:
15 MINUTES
PLUS CHILLING TIME

Strawberry and Peach Romanoff

SERVES 6	METRIC	IMPERIAL	AMERICAN
Strawberries, sliced	225 g	8 oz	8 oz
Peaches, stoned (pitted) and sliced	4	4	4
Caster (superfine) sugar	15 ml	1 tbsp	1 tbsp
Peach or orange liqueur	30 ml	2 tbsp	2 tbsp
Orange juice, freshly squeezed	45 ml	3 tbsp	3 tbsp
Whipped cream, to serve			

1 Put the prepared fruit in a glass bowl. Sprinkle with the sugar and pour the liqueur and orange juice over.

2 Leave to stand for 20–30 minutes before serving with whipped cream.

PREPARATION TIME:
10 MINUTES
PLUS STANDING TIME

Strawberry Syllabub

If you have time to chill this dessert for several hours before serving, it will separate into two luscious layers.

SERVES 6	METRIC	IMPERIAL	AMERICAN
Strawberries, hulled	350 g	12 oz	12 oz
Caster (superfine) sugar	100 g	4 oz	½ cup
Lemon juice	15 ml	1 tbsp	1 tbsp
Dry white wine	150 ml	¼ pt	⅔ cup
Double (heavy) cream	300 ml	½ pt	1¼ cups

1 Purée the fruit in a blender or processor.

2 Put the remaining ingredients in a bowl and whisk until softly peaking.

3 Fold in the strawberry purée gently with a metal spoon. Spoon into six wine goblets. Chill, if time allows, before serving.

PREPARATION TIME:
10 MINUTES
PLUS CHILLING TIME

Toffee Plum Charlotte

SERVES 4	METRIC	IMPERIAL	AMERICAN
Butter	50 g	2 oz	¼ cup
Light brown sugar	225 g	8 oz	1 cup
Lemon juice	15 ml	1 tbsp	1 tbsp
Thick slices of bread, cut from a large loaf	4	4	4
Ripe plums, quartered and stones (pits) removed	450 g	1 lb	1 lb
Double (heavy) cream, to serve			

1 Melt the butter in a large heavy-based frying pan (skillet). Add the sugar and stir over a gentle heat until the sugar has dissolved. Add the lemon juice.

2 Remove the crusts from the slices of bread and cut into cubes. Gently fold the bread cubes through the toffee mixture until completely coated. Add the plums, cover and cook for about 5 minutes until the fruit is soft.

3 Serve hot or chilled with thick cream.

PREPARATION TIME:
10–15 MINUTES

COOKING TIME:
8–10 MINUTES

Tropicana Delight

SERVES 4	METRIC	IMPERIAL	AMERICAN
Fresh pineapple	1	1	1
Fresh dates, quartered and stoned (pitted)	75 g	3 oz	½ cup
Small bananas, sliced	2	2	2
Light brown sugar	25 g	1 oz	2 tbsp
Apple juice	45 ml	3 tbsp	3 tbsp
Dark rum	45 ml	3 tbsp	3 tbsp

1 Cut the top off the pineapple about 3 cm/1½ in from the leaves and reserve to use as a lid.

2 Scoop out the pineapple flesh with a serrated knife, leaving the skin intact. Chop the flesh, discarding any hard core.

3 Put in a bowl with the dates and bananas. Toss lightly.

4 Blend together the sugar, apple juice and rum until the sugar has dissolved. Add to the bowl and toss well. Spoon the fruit and juice back into the pineapple shell, replace the lid and chill, if time allows, before serving.

PREPARATION TIME:
15 MINUTES
PLUS CHILLING TIME

Zabaglione

This dish was originally made with Marsala wine, but sweet sherry makes a very good alternative.

SERVES 4	METRIC	IMPERIAL	AMERICAN
Eggs	2	2	2
Caster (superfine) sugar	25 g	1 oz	2 tbsp
Sweet sherry	45 ml	3 tbsp	3 tbsp
Sponge (lady) fingers, to serve			

1 Put the ingredients in a deep bowl over a pan of hot water. Whisk until thick and creamy – a hand-held electric mixer is easiest, but a balloon whisk will give greater volume.

2 Pour the zabaglione into glasses and serve straight away with sponge fingers.

PREPARATION TIME:
5–10 MINUTES

QUICK BREADS, CAKES AND BISCUITS

Here is a miscellany of bakes, from appetising breads to serve with starters or main courses, through to tempting sweetmeats to serve with coffee. There are also some teatime treats to impress your family and friends.

Cornmeal Pancakes

Serve these with Quick Chilli (page 68), baked beans and grated cheese, crumbled bacon and scrambled egg, or any other savoury combination. Simply spoon on your chosen filling, roll up and eat with the fingers.

MAKES 8–10	METRIC	IMPERIAL	AMERICAN
Plain (all-purpose) flour	100 g	4 oz	1 cup
Salt	1.5 ml	¼ tsp	¼ tsp
Cornmeal	50 g	2 oz	½ cup
Water	375 ml	13 fl oz	1½ cups
Egg, beaten	1	1	1
Oil for greasing			

1 Whisk together all the ingredients in a bowl until smooth.

2 Heat a small, lightly oiled frying pan (skillet). Add about 45 ml/ 3 tbsp batter to coat the base thickly. Fry (sauté) over a moderate heat, swirling the pan gently until the pancake is dry but the edge is not brown. Turn over and cook the other side briefly.

3 Keep warm on a plate over a pan of hot water while cooking the remainder. Serve warm.

PREPARATION TIME: 10 MINUTES

COOKING TIME: ABOUT 30 MINUTES

Herby Pittas

SERVES 6	METRIC	IMPERIAL	AMERICAN
Pitta breads	3	3	3
Butter	65 g	2½ oz	good ¼ cup
Chopped mixed herbs (e.g. parsley, chives and marjoram)	30 ml	2 tbsp	2 tbsp
OR dried mixed herbs	15 ml	1 tbsp	1 tbsp
Garlic powder (optional)	5 ml	1 tsp	1 tsp

1 Halve the pittas widthways and split open along the cut edge to form pockets.

2 Mash together the butter and herbs with the garlic powder, if using. Spread inside the pockets.

3 Place under a hot grill (broiler) for 2 minutes on each side until the bread is crisp and golden and the butter has melted.

PREPARATION TIME:
5 MINUTES

COOKING TIME:
4 MINUTES (PITTAS)
15 MINUTES (LOAF)

Variation

Hot Herb Loaf: Make double the quantity of herb butter. Slice a small French stick into 12, not quite cutting through the bottom crust. Spread the butter mixture between the slices and over the top. Wrap in foil and bake in the oven at 200°C/400°F/gas mark 6 for about 15 minutes until the crust feels crisp when squeezed.

Hot Walnut Bread

SERVES 6	METRIC	IMPERIAL	AMERICAN
Walnut halves	*50 g*	*2 oz*	*½ cup*
Chopped parsley	*15 ml*	*1 tbsp*	*1 tbsp*
Butter	*50 g*	*2 oz*	*¼ cup*
Garlic salt	*2.5 ml*	*½ tsp*	*½ tsp*
Small French stick	*1*	*1*	*1*

1 Grind the nuts in a blender or processor. Add the remaining ingredients except the bread and blend well.

2 Cut the French stick into 12 slices, not quite slicing through the bottom crust. Spread the nut mixture between the slices and over the top.

3 Wrap in foil and bake in the oven at 200°C/400°F/gas mark 6 for 15 minutes until the crust feels crisp when squeezed.

PREPARATION TIME:
5 MINUTES

COOKING TIME:
15 MINUTES

Oatmeal Bannocks

MAKES 6	METRIC	IMPERIAL	AMERICAN
Wholemeal flour	175 g	6 oz	1½ cups
Baking powder	15 ml	1 tbsp	1 tbsp
Salt	2.5 ml	½ tsp	½ tsp
Fine oatmeal	50 g	2 oz	½ cup
Caster (superfine) sugar	15 ml	1 tbsp	1 tbsp
Margarine	25 g	1 oz	2 tbsp
Water	150 g	¼ pt	⅔ cup
Butter, to serve			

1 Mix together the dry ingredients, then rub in the margarine.

2 Mix with enough of the water to form a soft but not sticky dough. Knead gently and form into six flat cakes about 1 cm/½ in thick.

3 Cook on a griddle or in a hot non-stick frying pan (skillet) for about 5 minutes on each side until well risen and golden brown. Serve warm, split and buttered.

PREPARATION TIME:
10 MINUTES

COOKING TIME:
10 MINUTES

Quick Cheese Soda Bread

*If you run out of bread and want to make a quick plain loaf,
simply omit the cheese and mustard.*

MAKES 1 LOAF	METRIC	IMPERIAL	AMERICAN
Plain (all-purpose) flour	450 g	1 lb	4 cups
Bicarbonate of soda (baking soda)	10 ml	2 tsp	2 tsp
Cream of tartar	10 ml	2 tsp	2 tsp
Salt	5 ml	1 tsp	1 tsp
Mustard powder (optional)	2.5 ml	½ tsp	½ tsp
Butter or margarine	25 g	1 oz	2 tbsp
Strong Cheddar cheese, grated	100 g	4 oz	1 cup
Milk	300 ml	½ pt	1¼ cups
Butter, to serve			

1 Sift the dry ingredients into a bowl. Rub in the butter or margarine.

2 Stir in the cheese and enough of the milk to form a soft but not sticky dough.

3 Shape into a ball on a lightly floured surface.

4 Transfer to a baking sheet, flatten slightly and mark into quarters with a knife.

5 Bake in the oven at 220°C/425°F/gas mark 7 for 20–25 minutes until risen, golden and the base sounds hollow when tapped. Cool slightly, then break into quarters, slice thickly and serve with butter.

PREPARATION TIME:
10 MINUTES

COOKING TIME:
20–25 MINUTES

Rye Scotch Pancakes

MAKES ABOUT 24	METRIC	IMPERIAL	AMERICAN
Rye flour	100 g	4 oz	1 cup
Pinch of salt	1	1	1
Caster (superfine) sugar	10 ml	2 tsp	2 tsp
Eggs, separated	2	2	2
Milk	300 ml	½ pt	1¼ cups
Oil for shallow-frying			
Butter and honey, to serve			

1 Mix together the flour, salt and sugar.

2 Add the egg yolks and gradually beat in the milk.

3 Whisk the egg whites until peaking and fold into the batter with a metal spoon.

4 Heat a little oil in a large frying pan (skillet). Pour off the excess oil. Put tablespoonfuls of the batter into the pan a few at a time and cook on each side until golden. Keep warm in a clean cloth while cooking the remainder.

5 Serve warm with butter and honey.

PREPARATION TIME:
10 MINUTES

COOKING TIME:
ABOUT 20 MINUTES

Rum Truffle Cakes

These truffle cakes are perfect to serve with coffee after dinner, but are irresistible at any time.

MAKES 12	METRIC	IMPERIAL	AMERICAN
Golden (light corn) syrup	30 ml	2 tbsp	2 tbsp
Butter	25 g	1 oz	2 tbsp
Cocoa (unsweetened chocolate) powder	30 ml	2 tbsp	2 tbsp
Plain cake crumbs	100 g	4 oz	2 cups
Icing (confectioners') sugar	15 ml	1 tbsp	1 tbsp
Rum essence (extract)			
Cocoa (unsweetened chocolate) powder, to decorate			

1 Melt together the syrup, butter and cocoa powder. Stir in the cake crumbs, sugar and a few drops of rum essence to taste. The mixture should form a stiff paste. Roll into 12 small balls.

2 Chill for about 20 minutes, then roll in cocoa powder and place in sweet paper cases (candy cups). Store in the fridge.

PREPARATION TIME: 15 MINUTES PLUS CHILLING TIME

All-in-one Cake

MAKES ONE 18 CM/7 IN CAKE	METRIC	IMPERIAL	AMERICAN
Self-raising (self-rising) flour	175 g	6 oz	1½ cups
Baking powder	5 ml	1 tsp	1 tsp
Caster (superfine) sugar	175 g	6 oz	¾ cup
Soft margarine	175 g	6 oz	¾ cup

Jam (conserve) and a little extra caster sugar, to finish

1 Put all the ingredients in a processor and run the machine just until the mixture is blended and smooth, or put in a bowl and beat with a wooden spoon for about 2 minutes until smooth. Do not over-beat.

2 Grease two 18 cm/7 in sandwich tins (pans) and line the bases with baking parchment. Divide the mixture between the tins and level the surfaces.

3 Bake in the oven at 190°C/375°F/gas mark 5 for 20 minutes until risen, golden and the centres spring back when pressed. Turn out on to a wire rack to cool. Remove the paper.

4 Sandwich together with jam and sprinkle with a little caster sugar.

PREPARATION TIME:
10 MINUTES

COOKING TIME:
20 MINUTES

Variations

Chocolate: Substitute 25 g/1 oz/2 tbsp of the flour with cocoa (unsweetened chocolate) powder. Fill with whipped cream or chocolate spread.

Coffee: Dissolve 15 g/1 tbsp instant coffee granules in 15 ml/1 tbsp water and add to the basic mix. Sandwich with sweetened cream, flavoured with coffee liqueur or 5 ml/1 tsp coffee granules dissolved in 5 ml/1 tsp water.

Peanut Honey Bites

These biscuits make a quick and delicious teatime treat.

MAKES 12	METRIC	IMPERIAL	AMERICAN
Butter or margarine	75 g	3 oz	⅓ cup
Set honey	45 ml	3 tbsp	3 tbsp
Plain biscuits (cookies), crushed	225 g	8 oz	2 cups
Grated lemon rind	5 ml	1 tsp	1 tsp
Crunchy peanut butter	45 ml	3 tbsp	3 tbsp

1 Melt the butter or margarine with the honey and bring to the boil.

2 Stir in the remaining ingredients and mix well.

3 Press into a greased 18 cm/7 in square sandwich tin (pan) and chill until set. Cut into squares before serving.

PREPARATION TIME:
10 MINUTES
PLUS CHILLING TIME

Crispy Oatcake Thins

Perfect for breakfast, spread with butter and jam or marmalade, or served with cheese.

MAKES 8	METRIC	IMPERIAL	AMERICAN
Medium oatmeal	75 g	3 oz	¾ cup
Salt			
Bicarbonate of soda (baking soda)	1.5 ml	¼ tsp	¼ tsp
Butter, melted	15 g	½ oz	1 tbsp
Hot water	60 ml	4 tbsp	4 tbsp
Oil for greasing			

1 Put all the ingredients except the oil in a bowl and mix to a dough.

2 Turn out on to a surface dusted with oatmeal and pat or roll out thinly to about a 25 cm/10 in round.

3 Cut into eight wedges.

4 Lightly oil a large frying pan (skillet) and heat gently.

5 Cook the oatcakes a few at a time until firm. Turn over carefully so they don't break and cook for 2–3 minutes more. Cool on a wire rack. Store in an airtight tin.

PREPARATION TIME:
10 MINUTES

COOKING TIME:
4–6 MINUTES

Easy-does-it Biscuits

MAKES ABOUT 20	METRIC	IMPERIAL	AMERICAN
Soft butter or margarine	*65 g*	*2½ oz*	*good ¼ cup*
Caster (superfine) sugar	*50 g*	*2 oz*	*¼ cup*
Vanilla essence (extract)	*5 ml*	*1 tsp*	*1 tsp*
Self-raising (self-rising) flour	*100 g*	*4 oz*	*1 cup*

Whole blanched almonds or halved glacé (candied) cherries,
*   to decorate*

1 Put all the ingredients in a processor and run the machine just until the mixture forms a ball, or put in a bowl and work with a fork or wooden spoon until the mixture forms a ball.

2 Shape into walnut-sized balls and place a little apart on a greased baking sheet (you may need two). Press down with a fork dipped in cold water.

3 Bake in the oven at 190°C/375°F/gas mark 5 for 15 minutes until pale golden. Top each immediately with a nut or cherry half and leave for a few minutes to harden, then transfer to a wire rack to cool completely.

PREPARATION TIME: 10–15 MINUTES

COOKING TIME: 15 MINUTES

Muesli Cookies

MAKES ABOUT 30	METRIC	IMPERIAL	AMERICAN
Margarine	75 g	3 oz	⅓ cup
Light brown sugar	75 g	3 oz	⅓ cup
Golden (light corn) syrup	20 ml	4 tsp	4 tsp
Bicarbonate of soda (baking soda)	5 ml	1 tsp	1 tsp
Plain (all-purpose) flour	75 g	3 oz	¾ cup
Muesli	150 g	5 oz	1 cup

1 Melt the margarine, sugar and syrup in a pan. Add the bicarbonate of soda – it will froth up.

2 Stir in the flour and muesli. Shape into walnut-sized balls and place a little apart on two greased baking sheets. Flatten slightly with a fork.

3 Bake in the oven at 190°C/375°F/gas mark 5 for 8–10 minutes or until golden brown. Leave to cool for 2 minutes, then transfer to a wire rack to cool completely.

PREPARATION TIME:
10–15 MINUTES

COOKING TIME:
8–10 MINUTES

No-bake Chocolate Fudge Cakes

MAKES ABOUT 8	METRIC	IMPERIAL	AMERICAN
Butter or margarine	100 g	4 oz	½ cup
Icing (confectioners') sugar	175 g	6 oz	1 cup
Cocoa (unsweetened chocolate) powder	15 ml	1 tbsp	1 tbsp
Small chocolate fudge finger bars, cut into pieces	3	3	3
Plain sweet biscuits (cookies), crushed	175 g	6 oz	1½ cups
Mixed nuts, chopped	50 g	2 oz	½ cup
A little sifted icing (confectioners') sugar, to decorate			

1 Put the butter or margarine, cocoa and fudge fingers in a pan and heat gently, stirring, until melted.

2 Add the biscuits and nuts and mix well.

3 Turn into a greased 18 cm/7 in square sandwich tin (pan) and press down well. Leave to cool, then chill until set. Turn out on to a serving plate, dust with icing sugar and serve cut into fingers or squares.

PREPARATION TIME:
10 MINUTES
PLUS CHILLING TIME

INDEX